Henry Rains,
1767–1838

Henry Rains, 1767–1838

The Rains Family of Yellow Creek, Kentucky

David S. Rains

Writers Club Press

New York Lincoln Shanghai

Henry Rains, 1767–1838
The Rains Family of Yellow Creek, Kentucky

Writers Club Press
an imprint of iUniverse, Inc.

For information address:
iUniverse
2021 Pine Lake Road, Suite 100
Lincoln, NE 68512
www.iuniverse.com

ISBN: 0-595-25655-4 (Pbk)
ISBN: 0-595-65238-7 (Cloth)

Printed in the United States of America

Contents

Foreword

It is believed by many of the Rains family that we have Indian blood in our veins. After ten years of exhaustive research, I have found nothing to substantiate that claim. What I found, in old documents, deeds, marriage certificates, war records and wills, show that the **Rains men were Indian fighters instead of being Indians.** For example here are some reasons **I believe the Henry Rains family has no Indian blood:**

CHAPTER 1

Rains on Indian Lands and fighting Indians.

Henry Rains, 1767-1838, the first of our family in KY, fought against the Cherokee/Chickamauga with the Hawkins County Mounted Militia, under Captain John Blair in 1788. Two of his Lee stepbrothers served with him. **WHY WOULD HE FIGHT AGAINST THE INDIANS IF HE WERE ONE?**

Secondly, Henry's daughter, Mary Rains, and her husband Spencer King were in AL in 1818, attempting to squat on Indian lands. When the US Government told the settlers they would be removed for being there illegally, Spencer King signed a petition to the Secretary of War asking to be allowed to stay. The USA removed all the white settlers and Spencer King and his wife, Mary Rains King, returned to Knox County, KY. SEE any Knox County, KY, census from 1850 on, and you will see that Spencer King, Jr., was born in AL. **WHY WOULD THE USA REMOVE THEM FOR BEING WHITES IF THEY WERE INDIANS?** There were three petitions to stay on Indian Lands.

Marion County, TN., & Alabama Indian Lands PETITION TO STAY

"Copied from Record Group 75 obtained from the National Archives, Washington, D.C. and transcribed by Wanda Muncey Gant."

Memorial of the inhabitants residents in the Cherokee Country relative to the late order for their removal: To the Honorable the Secretary at War, Your petitioners viewing the calamitous situation in which many of our citizens are placed, owing to an order recently described by the agent for Indian affairs of the Cherokee Nation ordering all intruders on their lands to remove by the first day of July 1819. Your petitioners believing that the same indulgence would be extended to them as has been the constant practice to others in similar circumstances, induced them to settle on the lands lately ceded to the United States by the Cherokees on the north side of Tennessee River nor did the order ever appear until late in the month of May of this year, leaving a removal of the citizens impracticable if not impossible. Your petitioners are poor but industrious farmers and to deprive them of their hard earnings in the wilderness and thus destroy their labour, where will your petitioners apply for bread for their starving families; this order enforced will involve at least ONE THOUSAND families in total ruins, nor will the evil end here. Your petitioners must subsist somewhere & thus become unwelcome guests to the frontier counties to buy a little support for their starving children. The Indians are not desirous of having the intruders driven from this land North of Tennessee, those being few in numbers, & most of which have taken reservations and are good neighbors, your petitioners therefore knowing the lenity of their government and believing they will take our case into consideration will ever pray:

Doyal, T.
Hayter, J. J.
Tatton, Robert

Taylor, Joseph
Pryor, John
Trigg, Abram B.
Doughterty, John
Dixan, W. D.
Burritt, W.
McKinney, Thomas
Henderson, A.
Burton, R.
Young, Joseph Jr.
Clayton, R. B.
Klepper, Powel
Buttute, Thomas
Estill, Isaac
Lewis, Henderson
Yuddeuth, Samuel
Estill, John
Hill, James
Raines, William M. (I believe this to be the Rains who moved to AL)
Dickson, James
Wilson, Zacheus
Robinson, W. H.
McLaughlin, Wm. B.
Brittain, William
Kinningham, William
Robinson, Jonas
Bradford, Benjamin M.
Sharp, Robert P.
Key, John
Kidder, Holbert
Moor, James
Street, Wm.

Eangs, Daniel
Hays, William
Harrall, Whitefield
Saxton, Alexander
Seykes, John (John SYKES)
Matthews, John
Mann, Mathew R.
McLaughlin, William
Suddarth, Dyer
McMillin, E. K.
Hardwicke, J.
Paschal, William
Cathching, Meredith
Slone, Samuel C.
___, J.
Hill, John or M.
Hill, Thomas
Hill, Joseph
Hill, John Sr.
Hill, Mitchell L.
Burress, William
Mahony, Denis
Farris, Ricard
Shelton, Peter
Hill, Thomas M. [marked out]
Tally, Lewis B. [Tully?]
Reeves, Wm.
Lea, Wm. W.
Bradford, Jos. H.
Has___s?, S. W.
Miner, Samuel
Tarrant, Leonard

Snead, Richard
Price, Euagey
Reaves, Abner
Russey, Benjamin
Barre__, Jeremiah
Embrey, Wiley S.
Branagan, John J.
Bacon, Thos. [Barns?]
Jones, J. W.
Estill, Wallis
Howell, Thomas
Cowan, Samuel M.
Harris, Mark M.
Rainey, Benj. A.
Frazier, Thompson
Cock, Lester
Wiggin, J. P. [Duggen?]
Ellis, Ellison
Townsend, Joshua
Townsend, Ozra
Blagg, Israel
Townsend, Thomas
Townsend, John
Hutton, John
Hutton, William
Williams, Thomas
Jenkins, Richard
Bost, Thomas
Johnson, Jacob Sr.
Johnson, Reuben
King, Allen (Probable father of Spencer King)
Walker, Edward

Williams, David
Gilliland, James
Davidson, H. M.
Davidson, George
Woods, Peter
Davidson, William
Davidson, John P.
Williams, Alexander Jr.
Frost, Joseph
Williams, Theoples
Frost, Thomas
Looney, Isam
Looney, John
Erwin, George
Williams, Alexander [marked out]
Blevins, Elisha
Blevins, John
Johnston, John
Acton, John
Sullivan, J. H.

_____,_____

Crafford, Adam
Bird, John
Freeman, Johnson
Bird, George
Garrison, Joseph
Garrison, James
Looney, Jessee
Looney, Isaac
Looney, Absolum
Looney, Benjamin
Looney, Allen

Looney, Benjamin
Looney, William G.

2nd Petition To the Honorable the Secretary at War: Your petitioners viewing the calamatious situation in which many of our citizens are placed owing to an order recently published by the agent for Indian affairs of the Cherokee Nation **ordering all intruders on their land to remove by the first day of July 1819.** Your petitioners believing the same indulgence would be extended to them, as has been the constant practice to others in similar circumstances, **induced them to settle** on the lands lately ceded to the United States by the Cherokees north of Tennessee River, nor did the order ever make its formal appearance until the 19th of June of the present year leaving a removal impracticable if not impossible. Your petitioners are poor but industrious farmers to deprive them at this season of the year of their hard earnings in the wilderness and thus leave them destitute where will your petitioners apply for bread to support their starving families? It is notorious that all improvements made by your petitioners add real value to the land, this order enforced, will, involve at least ONE THOUSAND families in total ruin! Nor will the evil end here. Your petitioners must subsist somewhere, they will thus become unwelcome guests to the frontier counties to beg [for they cannot buy] something for their little children. This measure if carried into operation will produce alarming effects. The Indians on the North of Tennessee are not desirous of having the settlers driven off the land, those being few in number, most of which have taken reservations and are good neighbours. Your petitioners knowing the lenity of their government and believing they will take our case into consideration will ever pray:

Burks, Isham Sr.
Burks, Wm.

Burks, John
Thurman, John
Burks, Charles
Burks, Isham Jr.
Forbush, Absalem
Meek, Jacob
Meek, Henery
Saxon, Robert
Saxon, Robert Jr.
Cargile, Lewis
Camron?, Danel
Couch, Moses
Couch, Lindley
Bond, Jesse
Bond, Benjamin
Looney, John
Woodson, Abraham
Brock, Jesee
Woodson, David
Jonston, Jacob
Crawford, Joseph
Crawford, David
Corbit, Benjamin
Boss, Meth_____ [Bass?]
Johnson, Benjamin
Cox, Abel
Morris, Robert
Jenkins, William
Jenkins, Joshua
Woodson, Shadrach
Goode, Joseph
Jenkins, Joseph

Thornton, William
Corbit, Charles
Corbit, Thomas
Garrison, Isaac
Byrd, Ca____
Mullins, Washington
Parker, Robert

3rd petition
Mullin, Swift
Schrimshear, William
Underwood, Benjamin
Berry, John
Forbes, Daniel
Hall, James
Neeley, H. N.
Jones, John
Gaily, James
Rentfro, Robert
Maxwell, John
Oban, Robert
King, Spencer (married Mary Rains, daughter of Henry Rains, 1767–1838)
Stephens, William
Cage, Valentine
Brisco, Thomas
Brisco, James
Brisco, Wiliam
Bire, George
Dawson, William
Hawks, Moses
Lollar, James

Johnson, John
Williams, Bryant
Scott, William
Allen, Wilson
Price, Kinchen
Wimberly, Joel
Martin, David
Scott, Samuel
Lollar, Jacob
Price, John
Harmon, Mark
Sides, Levi
Schrimshear, James
Williams, Wiley
Price, Edwin
Lollar, Isaach
Lollar, Henry
Lollar, John
Bird, Benjamin
Bird, Valentine
Bird, John Jr.
Williams, Alexander
Williams, Lewis
Williams, Bryant
Canada, Quate
Rutherford, James
Charles, Oliver
Williams, James
Thornton, William
Watken, James H.
Miller, Alexander
Brown, William

Brown, Alexander
Blanchet, Peter
McQueen, David C.
Murry, Robert
Thornton, Joseph
Thornton, Clark
Corbit, Charles
Kelly, Mathew
Lynch, Eligh
Blevins, Jonathan
Lewis, John
Young, Joseph
Cain, Daniel R.?
Acton, John
Allen, Wilson
Bacon, Thos.
Barrett, Jeremiah
Bass, Mit
Berry, John
Bird, Benjamin
Bird, George
Bird, John Jr.
Bird, John
Bird, Valentine
Bire, George
Blagg, Israel
Blanchet, Peter
Blevins, Elisha
Blevins, John
Blevins, Jonathan
Bond, Benjamin
Bond, Jesse

Bost, Thomas
Bradford, Benjamin M.
Bradford, Jos. H.
Branagan, John J.
Brisco, James
Brisco, Thomas
Brisco, Wiliam
Brittain, William
Brock, Jesee
Brown, Alexander
Brown, William
Burks, Charles
Burks, Isham Jr.
Burks, Isham Sr.
Burks, John
Burks, Wm.
Burress, William
Burritt, W.
Burton, R.
Buttrite, Thomas
Byford, _____
Cage, Valentine
Canada, Quate
Cargile, Lewis
Carsson?, Danel
Cathching, Meredith
Charles, Oliver
Clayton, R. B.
Cock, Lester
Corbit, Benjamin
Corbit, Charles
Corbit, Charles

Corbit, Thomas
Couch, Lindley
Couch, Moses
Cowan, Samuel M.
Cox, Abel
Crafford, Adam
Crawford, David
Crawford, Joseph
Davidson, George
Davidson, H. M.
Davidson, John P.
Davidson, William
Dawson, William
Dickson, James
Dixan, W. D.
Doughterty, John
Doyal, T.
Eanes, Daniel
Ellis, Ellison
Embrey, Wiley S.
Erwin, George
Estill, Isaac
Estill, Wallis
Farris, Ricard
Forbush, Absalem
Forkes, Daniel
Frazier, Thompson
Freeman, Johnson
Frost, Joseph
Frost, Thomas
Gaily, James
Garrison, Isaac

Garrison, James
Garrison, Joseph
Gilliland, James
Goode, Joseph
Hall, James
Hardwicke, J.
Harmon, Mark
Harrall, Whitefield
Harris, Mark M.
Harris?, S. W.
Hawks, Moses
Hays, William
Hayter, J. J.
Henderson, A.
Hill, James
Hill, John Sr.
Hill, John _
Hill, Joseph
Hill, Mitchell L.
Hill, Thomas
Hill, Thomas M. [marked out]
Howell, Thomas
Hutton, John
Hutton, William
Jenkins, Joshua
Jenkins, Jospeh
Jenkins, Richard
Jenkins, William
Johnson, Benjamin
Johnson, Jacob Sr.
Johnson, John
Johnson, Reuben

Johnston, John
Jones, J. W.
Jones, John
Jonston, Jacob
Kelly, Mathew
Key, John
Kindder, Holbert
King, Allen
King, Spencer
Kinningham, William
Klepper, Powel _
Lea, Wm. W.
Lewis, John
Lollar, Henry
Lollar, Isaach
Lollar, Jacob
Lollar, James
Lollar, John
Looney, Absolum
Looney, Allen
Looney, Benjamin
Looney, Benjamin
Looney, Isaac
Looney, Isam
Looney, Jessee
Looney, John
Looney, John
Looney, William G.
Lynch, Eligh
Mahony, Denis
Mann, Mathew R.
Martin, David

Matthews, John
Maxwell, John
McGQueen, David C.
McKinney, Thomas [Kinney?]
McLaughlin, William
McLaughlin, Wm. B.
McMillin, E. K.
Meek, Henery
Meek, Jacob
Miller, Alexander
Miner, Samuel
Moor, James
Morris, Robert
Mullin, Swifte
Mullins, Washington
Murry, Robert
Neeley, H. N.
Oban, Robert
Parker, Robert
Paschal, William
Price, Edwin
Price, Euagey
Price, John
Price, Kinchen
Pryor, John?
Raines, William M.
Rainey, Benj. A.
Reaves, Abner
Reeves, Wm.
Rentfro, Robert
Robinson, Jonas
Robinson, W. H.

Russey, Benjamin
Rutherford, James
Saxon, Robert Jr.
Saxon, Robert
Saxton, Alexander
Schrimshear
Schrimshear, William
Scott, Samuel
Scott, William
Seykes, John (**John SYKES**)
Sharp, Robert P.
Shelton, Peter
Sides, Levi
Slone, Samuel C.
Snead, Richard
Stephens, William
Street, Wm.
Suddarth, Dyer
Sullivan, J. _
Tarrant, Leonard
Tatton, Robert
Taylor, Joseph
Thornton, Clark
Thornton, Joseph
Thornton, William
Thornton, William
Thurman, John
Townsend, John
Townsend, Joshua
Townsend, Ozra
Townsend, Thomas
Trigg, Abram B.

Tully, Lewis B. [Tally?]
Underwood, Benjamin
Walker, Edward
Walker, James H.
Wiggin, J. P.
Williams, Alexander Jr.
Williams, Alexander
Williams, Alexander [marked out]
Williams, Bryant
Williams, Bryant
Williams, David
Williams, James
Williams, Lewis
Williams, Theoples
Williams, Thomas
Williams, Wiley
Wilson, Zacheus
Wimberly, Joel
Woods, Peter
Woodson, Abraham
Woodson, David
Woodson, Shdrach
Young, Joseph
Young?, Joseph Jr.
Cain, Daniel R.?

"Permanent publication rights granted to TNGenNet Inc."

Author's note: Before the Cherokee ceded their lands to the USA, Agents recruited settlers to settle the former Indian lands, in violation of the Cherokee treaty. Thus, the order to remove the illegal settlers. **As to proper language, grammar and spelling,** I have tried to leave the original language that was in the document without changes. Where Spelling and word use were so bad as to cause mis-interpretation of meanings, I have tried to correct it without changing the intent.

Third, the Rains family married into the Turner family. The Turners were notorious Indian haters due to several of their women being killed by the Cherokee in the last Indian uprising in TN. A Professor Turner wrote the book that set Andrew Jackson on the path to Indian removal, under the theory of "Manifest Destiny." That book said the Indians did not deserve to own land…No Indian was allowed to own land, vote, or marry a white person until the early 1900s in KY. All Indians were made Citizens of the USA in 1924. The Rains family could not have been Indian any more than the Turners could have been. SEE: The US Supreme Court decisions called "The Marshall Trilogy." **Discovery Law**

JOHNSON v. M'INTOSH, 21 U.S (8 Wheat) 543 (1823). This case involved a dispute between two white men who held con-flicting titles to land sold within the reservation to them. Johnson held a title sold him by the Tribe within the reserva-tion. Chief Justice Marshall, examined the history of how land was acquired during the European invasion and ultimately held that the tribe did not have an enforceable title to the land it sold. The Indians enjoyed a right of "occupancy" only. The ultimate title to land had passed to the United States govern-ment under a principle called "discovery."

The "discovery doctrine" was developed by the Spanish philosopher, Vittorio, in an attempt to justify and explain the taking of land from aboriginal people. In its essence, Vittorio opined that it was the manner in which the civilized nations dealt with each other as it pertained to the land, that gov-erned who had title. A European nation that discovered land occupied by aboriginal people, assumed certain rights over that land that were recognized by the other European nations. It was these "recognized" rights that were passed on to the United States when it won the War of Independence. I will not attempt to go on a further dissertation on the doctrine, except to say that, in it, Marshall found the rationale for asserting federal title power over the land versus state power. As a result, with the adoption of the "discovery doctrine," the Court held the title to land passed to the plaintiff by the Illinois and Piankeshaw tribes was invalid because Indians held only a title of <u>occupancy, and not full title.</u>

While it is true that two Rains people married Indians in the middle 1800s, in Georgia, they were not a part of the Henry Rains, 1767-1838, family, nor were they part of the John Turner of Knox County, KY, family. Henry Rains and John Turner, Sr., came from old English privileged North Carolina stock.

As further proof of the Rains family' attitude toward Indians, I offer this petition sent to VA for a new and closer courthouse. Three Rains men sign it.

<u>KY: Petitions of the Early Inhabitants of KY to the Gen Assembly of VA</u>
1769-92 James Robertson 1914

KY was a county of VA until 1792, when it became a State.

Petitions of the people of Limestone (Bourbon Co, KY)

"…subject to much danger inconvenience and expense; in having to attend their transactions of their County business at the distance of forty miles from their habitations (for the most part surrounded with all the horrors of a Savage Enemy.)"

....(3rd paragraph)"Your Petitioners humbly observe that Twelve or fifteen miles of the way they must travil to their Courthouse is thro a Barren Country unfit for Cultivation that this aggrevates their danger as it is and may remain a secure Asylum to the Savages who infest the road, that for the most part it is unsafe to travil it in the Summer time unless in Companies of armed men, and that in the winter time, the journey to or from Court cannot be perform'd in much less time than two daies, And that there are several considerable & rapid water courses, which often obstructs a convenient communication with the other part of the sd County. Which renders their attendance at Court extremely expensive & inconvenient, that they are often under the indispensible obligations of attending Court being subject as they become freeholders to attend on Grand Juries & other necessary duties which as Citizens they are liable to. That from being so much expos'd to the inroads of the Savages they have not a horse left for every tenth man..."

Signers includes **Cornelius Rains**

John Rains

William Rains

They are asking that a new county be formed and a courthouse closer to them. They want to name their new community "Washington"

This small community had 50 families (on 700 acres?) 1787 in Bourbon Co KY

The group petitioned the Va legislature several times

1. The first petition was signed by **James Rains, John Rains, William Rains**

2. Signed by **Cornelius Rains, James Rains, John Rains, and Wm.Rains.**

3. Signed by Cornelius, and John and William Rains

4. Signed by Cornelius, John and William Rains

While it is true that many Cherokee took American names, such as "Turner" and "Anderson," that does not mean they were in fact related to any Turner, Anderson or any other white family. It simply means they took American names. The freed slaves did the same after the Civil War, by taking the names of their former masters. **SEE:** 1860 Knox County Census, **George Rains and family,** who are all **"Mulattoes"** and "freed slaves of the Rains family." The fact they are of mixed blood suggests they are related to the White Rains families of Knox County, KY.

CHAPTER 2

English Roots of Surname Rains

As to whether or not the Rains family descends from Englishmen, I offer the research of Dr. Thomas Hart Rains, MD, of VA: **RAINS MEN-TIONED IN DOMESDAY BOOK**

A General Introduction to the Domesday Book by Sir Henry Ellis, Vols 1 & 2, abstract Gen Pub Co 1973 from 1833 edition.

p. 473 lists Rogerius de Rames of Middlesex 130 b.v.

p. 473 Ramis—Rogerus de Ramis; In villa de Gepesuiz habet Rogeris E. ecclesiam S. Georgii et IIII burgenses et VI. uastatas mansueras

Volume II p. 374 (Survey of Persons and Monasteries, etc.) Rogerus de Ramis, Essex 6 b 14 b 87 b Norf 214 Suff 352 b 3 93 b

Key to the Ancient Parish Registers of England and Wales by Arthur Meredyth Burker 1962 Gen Pub Co London 1908, p. 130

Name Area earliest date

Rayne Essex 1558

Rainford Lanc 1718

Rainham Kent 1592

Essex 1570

Rainham East Norf. 1627

"West" 1539

"South" 1740

Rainow Chest. 1765

Rame Cornwall 1653

p. 40

Aldborough York 1538

Norfolk 1539

Aldburgh York 1653

The Agincourt Honor Rolls, of those who fought for King Henry V in France, 1415 AD.

John Reynes. Allied names, John De Massy, William Massy, John Massy De Preston.

As **further evidence of English descent** I offer the following list of Judges against the Protestant "Heretics," who heard evidence against the Protestants on behalf of the Crown.

Protestant Dissenters & Those who judged them, 1607-1691, in England:
Barlow, Thomas, 1607-1691 Several miscellaneous and weighty cases of conscience : learnedly and judiciously resolved / by the Right Reverend Father in God, Dr. Thomas Barlow, late Lord-Bishop of Lincoln Viz. I. Of toleration of Protestant dissenters. II. The king's power to pardon murder. III. Objections from Gen. 9.6 answered. IV. Mr. Cottington's case of divorce: with the judgments of Dr. Allestrey, Dr. Hall, Sir Richard Lloyd, **Sir Richard Raines**, Dr. Oldys, and the Doctors of the Sorbonne, upon the same. V. For toleration of the Jews. VI. About setting up images in churches. VII. An dominium fundatur in gratia? With two pages omitted in the English Machiavel, and his lordship's censure thereupon. Printed, and sold by Mrs. Davis : London , **1692** CLASS NO.: K 3280 B37 1692 <4>, 93, 40, 14, 134, 78, 46, <1>, 1 port. ; 18 cm. (8vo) Ref.: Wing, B 843 **Author's Note: It was customary in England to have several Noblemen on any Church Court, to represent the King.**

HEDGES, SIR CHARLES (1649–1714), lawyer and politician, great-grandson of John Lacy of Wiltshire, was son of Henry Hedges of Wanborough in that County' who married Margaret, daughter of R Pleydell of Childers, Berkshire; Sir William Hedges [q. v.3 was his second cousin. He was educated at Oxford, taking the degrees of B.A. 29 Nov. 1670, when he was at Magdalen Hap; M.A. (of Magdalen College) on 31 May 1673, and D.C.L. on 26 June 1675. On 25 Oct. in the last year he was admitted to the Society of Advocates; he was created chancellor and vicar-general of the diocese of Rochester by patent for life in 1686, and master of the faculties and judge of the admiralty court, in place of **Sir Richard Raines, on 1 June 1689,** when he was also knighted. He was returned as M.P. for Oxford n Suffolk in 1698, but counter-petitions for and against the return were presented. Hedges and his colleagues were unseated by an election committee (1 Feb. 1700), and the house confirmed the decision by a majority of one vote (10 Feb.) In the short-lived parliament of 1701 he sat for Dover, and at the election in November 1701 he was returned for Calne and Malmesbury. His opponents endeavoured to eject him from both places, and the election for Calne was declared void, but the petition against his return for Malmesbury failed. At the next election (August 1703) he was again returned for both Calne and Malmesbury, and in this instance elected to serve for the former borough. He contested the constituency of Calne again in 1705 and 1708, but was not successful. He nevertheless retained a seat in parliament, as he was thrice (1705, 1708, 1710) returned for West Looe, and once (1713) for East Looe. His political opinions were those of the Tories, but he usually voted as his own individual interest prompted. Mainly through the influence of the Earl of Rochester he was sworn as secretary of state and a privy councillor on 5 Nov. 1700, when, according to Luttrell, he was allowed by special permission of the king to remain judge of the admiralty court, and he continued to be judge until 29 Dec. 1701. The Duchess of Marlborough said of him: He has no capacity, no quality nor interest, nor ever could have been in that post [i.e. the secretaryship] but that everybody knows my Lord Rochester cares for nothing, so much as a man that he thinks will depend upon him' (Account of Conduct of Duchess of Marlborough, pp. 204-11. He attended the queen to Bath in August 1702, and for a short time (April to May 1704) he was declared the sole secretary, both home and foreign, until a successor was appointed to the Earl of Nottingham. During 1706 the Whigs constantly endeavored to eject him from office to make room for the Earl of Sunderland, and the queen at last submitted. The change was announced on 8 Dec. 1706, but it was stipulated that Hedges should be appointed to the judgeship of the pre-rogative court of Canterbury on its vacation by **Sir Richard Raines**, and in January 1711 he succeeded to that post. In November of the same year he was mentioned as the third plenipotentiary to negotiate the treaty of Utrecht, but it never passed beyond rumor. For some time his chief residence was at Richmond Green, in a house which afterwards passed to Sir Matthew Decker, but in 1700 he bought the estate of Compton Camberwell, in Compton Bassett, near Calne, and the family arms are still preserved around the parapet of the house. He owned much property in Wiltshire. Among the privately printed works of Sir Thomas Phillipps was one called 'Land-holders of Wanborough; from a Map of Wanborough, the estate of the Right Hon. Sir Charles Hedges. Taken and drawn in 1709 by P. Assenton.' Hedges died on 10 June 1714, and was buried at Wanborough on 15 June. His widow, Eleanor, daughter of George Smith, a proctor in London, died in 1733, and was also buried at Wanborough. They had issue one daughter and three sons, Henry, William, and Charles. William married as his first wife Elizabeth, sole heiress of the family of Gore, at Alderton in Wiltshire (cf. Gent. Mag. 1836, pt. i p. 376, and Aubrey, Collections, ed. the Rev. J E. Jackson, p. 46).

Hedges is said to have been the anonymous author of ' Reasons for Setling (sic) Admiralty Jurisdiction and giving encourage-ment to Merchants, Owners, Masters of Ships, Material Men, and Marines,' 1690, the main object of which was to improve the methods of pressing seamen. Henry Maundrell was his nephew, and the famous 'Journey from Aleppo, to Jerusalem at Easter 1697 'is dedicated to him. Hearne records in his diary that Hedges gave this book to the university, but that the offi-cials were guilty of some discourtesy that displeased the donor.

At the sale of the library of the College of Advocates at Doctors' Commons there were purchased for the British Museum the Addit. MSS. 24102-07, all relating to Hedges. They contain notes of cases heard by him, accounts of his fees, with cases and precedents that he had collected. The most interesting is his letter-book (No. 24107), comprising copies of his letters, official and private, including many to Maundrell. Many other letters to and from him are at the British Museum and in the collections described in the Historical Manuscripts Commission. His grand-daughter was mother of Colonel Montagu, the ornithologist, after whose death upwards of three hundred letters written to Hedges by the first Duke of Marlborough, and three notes addressed to him by Queen Anne, were sold at auction in 1816 for 670 guineas. Some letters from Marlborough to him are printed in Murray's ' Letters and Dispatches of the Duke.' Elkanah Settle issued in 1714 a funeral poem to the memory of Hedges.

Secretary Hedges

Next in authority to the chancellor and the treasurer were the secretaries of state. That office had evolved from the personal secretary of the king into a great office during the reign of Henry VIII, but the secretaries were still regarded as peculiarly the queen's personal servants. Queen Anne for example asked Sir Charles Hedges to "send me some good pens, for those I have are soe bad I can hardly make them writt."

The secretaries were expected to wait on the Queen daily, or if absent from London to attend to her in rotation while traveling. They would have to move their staff and duties with them as they traveled. The duties as secretary also involved domestic and foreign administration.

The kingdom was divided into the northern and southern departments, and the diplomatic relations with foreign countries also divided, including the control of diplomatic corps. Domestic administration was handled through the lords lieutenants of the various counties, generally great landowners from each neighborhood.

The Queen acted as the final court of appeal, and wrote to Sir Charles Hedges about one condemned convict " having a wife and six children, makes me think it is a case of compassion; however I desire you would inform yourself about it as soon as you can possible, and if you find it soe, take care his life may be spared.

Earl of Nottingham Daniel Finch refused to become secretary of state unless the Tory loyalist, Sir Charles Hedges, was to replace secretary James Vernon. Vernon described himself as "too obnoxious to the Tory party to continue" and took his ample pension.

I beleeve Mr. Secretary Hedges to be too honest a man to say any man was a good man if he did not know him to be soe. I know ye people ye beleeve have not this opinion of him soe that I feare my Character of him will not be credited...

The above testimonial of Secretary Hedges resulted from a argument about the influence that the Tories might have had upon Queen Anne, the opposition of which was endeavoring to replace all Tories with the Whigs in all government positions.

The Junto, (Whigs) being flush with newly acquired power, demanded the replacement of Mr. Secretary Harley, to make way for their own, young Earl of Sunderland, who was also the husband of the Queen's namesake goddaughter, Lady Anne Churchill. This group soon found Sir Charles Hedges a much less formidable target, as he was described as " has noe capasity, noe quality, no interest, nor never could have been in that post, but that…Lord Rochester cares for nothing so much as a man that hee thinks will depend upon him.

Queen Anne opposed Sunderland, and intended to make the government a cooperative group rather than in the control of extremist from either side, Whig or Tory.

Godolphin assured the Queen that the change would not work a hardship upon Sir Charles Hedges, who had expressed an interest to retire. Queen Anne was emotionally opposed to the appointment of Sunderland as secretary, but after many months of "hurly burly" was wearing down, and shifting friends away from those who sought to encourage her.

The price of Sunderlands appointment, which called for the dismissal of Mr Secretary Hedges in the December Parliament of 1706 was support by the Whigs for the ongoing war. Secretary Harley feared for his own job, since he was the original target, and dropped his opposition to Sunderland.

Sir Charles Hedges was promised the first vacancy in the prerogative Court of Canterbury, for which he had to wait until January 1711.

Queen Anne by Edward Gregg, 1980, Routledge & Kegen Paul.

Names of MILITARY MEN trained and ready to be deployed for any landing on England by the Spanish:

1588		
Acres	___, Captain—BRISTOLE Corporal of the Field	To Attend Lord Hundson
Allen	Captain—BRISTOLE	
Arden	Commissary of the Vituals	
Barnishe	Captain	To Attend Earl of Leicester
Barton	Captain	To Attend Earl of Leicester
Bealinge	Captain—LIVERPOOLE	
Berkeley	Edward, Captain	
Berkeley	Henry, **Sir**	To Attend Lord Hundson
Bingham	John, Captain—WARWICK	
Bourchier	George, **Sir**	
Bowes	Jerome, **Sir**	
Brereton	Captain	To Attend Earl of Leicester
Careles (Alias Wright)	Captain	To Attend Earl of Leicester
Carew	Roger, Captain	To Attend Lord Hundson
Carey	George, 2nd Baron Hundson, Lord Chamberlain & Lieutenant General of Defence, Captain of the Isle in 1590	Assemble at St James to protect the Queen
Carlel	Captain	
Carleton	George, Captain	
Champernoun	Gawen, Captain	
Christmas	Captain	To Attend Earl of Leicester
Cooke	Captain	To Attend Earl of Leicester
Couper	John—BRISTOLE	
Crewes	Captain	

Cripse	Captain—Provost Marshall	
Cunstable	Robert, **Sir**—Master of the Ordinance	Assemble at St James to protect the Queen
Dawtry	Nicholas, Captain—Sergeant Major	To Attend Earl of Leicester
Devereaux	Robert, 2nd Earl of Essex, General	Assemble at St James to protect the Queen
De L'Espine (Spindola)	Phillip, Captain—WARWICK	
Doudall	Captain	To Attend Lord Hundson
Drury	H, Captain	
Dudley	Robert, Lord Lieutenant General, Earl of Leicester	
Dudley	Captain	To Attend Earl of Leicester
Ellis	Captain—WILTSHIRE	
Finche	Molie, **Sir**—Treasurer & deputy to Sir Thomas Hennadge	
Fitzwilliams	Brian	
Fitzwilliams	William, **Sir**	
Goodwine	William—BRISTOLE	
Goodyear	Henry, **Sir**	To Attend Earl of Leicester
Goodyeare	Henry, **Sir**—LIVERPOOLE	
Gorge	Thomas, **Sir**	
Goringe	Captain—LIVERPOOLE	To Attend Earl of Leicester
Gray of Wilton	Lord Marshall	Assemble at St James to protect the Queen
Grenville	Richard, Captain	To Attend Lord Hundson
Harrington	Henry, **Sir**	
Harte	Captain—LIVERPOOLE	To Attend Earl of Leicester
Hastings	Edward, **Sir**	
Hennadge	Thomas, **Sir**—Treasurer	Assemble at St James to protect the Queen

Henworthe	Captain	To Attend Lord Hundson
Highefield	Captain	
Hitchcock	Captain	
Hoord	Captain	To Attend Lord Hundson
Huntley	Captain—LIVERPOOLE	
Hussey	Roger—LIVERPOOLE	To Attend Earl of Leicester
Jenibelli	Federico, Captain—Trench Master	
Judge	Captain	To Attend Earl of Leicester
Knolleys	Francis, **Sir**—Master of the Ordinance & Colonel General of the Foot, Treasurer of the Household	Assemble at St James to protect the Queen
Knyvet	Henry, **Sir**	To Attend Lord Hundson
Lane	**Ralph, Captain—Muster Master**	To Attend Earl of Leicester **Had been Governor at Roanoke, cousin to Queen Elizabeth**
Latham	Captain	To Attend Earl of Leicester
Leighton	Thomas, **Sir**—Colonel General of the Footmen	
Ley	Henry, **Sir**	
Manners	Thomas, **Sir**	
Marchant	Captain	
Marckham	Thomas	
Merreman	Captain	
Moore	Edward, **Sir**—LIVERPOOLE	To Attend Earl of Leicester
Moore	G, Captain	
Morgan	Thomas—SOMERSET	
Newton	Captain	
Newton	Captain	

Norris	Henry, **Sir**	To Attend Earl of Leicester
Norris	John, **Sir**, Lord Marshall, 2nd in Command	Assemble at St James to protect the Queen
North	Roger, Lord North, Captain of the Lighthorse	Assemble at St James to protect the Queen
Palmer	Henry, **Sir**	
Parkinson	Captain	To Attend Lord Hundson
Paulet	Hambden, Captain—LIVERPOOLE	
Peacock	Captain	To Attend Earl of Leicester
Petty	Edmond, Captain—Scout Master	To Attend Earl of Leicester
Philpott	Edward—BRISTOLE	To Attend Earl of Leicester
Piper	Captain	To Attend Earl of Leicester
Plott	Captain	
Price	Captain	
Radcliffe	Thomas, Earl of Sussex, Captain of Portsmouth, Isle of Wight (1590)	
Raines	Captain	To Attend Earl of Leicester
Raleigh	Walter, **Sir**	
Read	William, **Sir**—Serjant Major	Assemble at St James to protect the Queen
Riggs	John, Captain—LIVERPOOLE	
Roberts	John, Captain—WARWICK	
Roper	John, Captain	To Attend Earl of Leicester
Roper	Thomas—BRISTOLE	
Scudamore	Captain	
Selby	William, Captain	
Shute	Captain	To Attend Lord Hundson
Sidenham		

Sidney	Robert, Sir, Captain of the Lighthorse	
Smithe	John, **Sir**	To Attend Lord Hundson
Spencer	James, Lt—Lt. To the Master of the ordinance, Francis Knolleys	
Stanley	Edward, **Sir**	
Staunton	Captain, the elder—WILTSHIRE	To Attend Lord Hundson
Staunton	Captain, the younger—WILTS	To Attend Lord Hundson
Strange	_____—BRISTOLE	
Sucklif	Edmond, Captain - Judge of the Army	
Tanner	Captain	To Attend Earl of Leicester
Trevit/ Tyrwhitt	Tristram, Captain	To Attend Lord Hundson
Turner	Captain	To Attend Lord Hundson
Twittie / Tutty	Captain	To Attend Earl of Leicester
Vaughn	John	
Waldegrave	Captain	To Attend Earl of Leicester
Warde	Captain	
Watts	John, Captain	To Attend Lord Hundson
West	Thomas—BRISTOLE	
Westrope	Captain	To Attend Earl of Leicester
Wheeler	Captain	To Attend Lord Hundson
Williams	Roger, Sir, Captain of the Lances	To Attend Earl of Leicester
Wilson	Captain—Corporal of the Field	To Attend Lord Hundson
Wingfield	Anthony,—LIVERPOOLE	To Attend Lord Hundson
Wingfield	Edward, **Sir**	To Attend Lord Hundson
Woodhouse	Captain—LIVERPOOLE	To Attend Lord Hundson
Woolfe	Morgan—LIVERPOOLE	To Attend Earl of Leicester
Wright	See Carelas	

Yorke	Edmond—LIVERPOOLE—Quarter Master	To Attend Earl of Leicester
Yorke	Edward, Captain—BRISTOLE	To Attend Lord Hundson
Yorke	Gilbert, Captain	

CHAPTER 3

Raines Roots in America

THE 16TH CENTURY

In 1587, 117 men, women, and children set foot on a New World. Their benefactor, <u>Sir Walter Raleigh</u>, had long dreamed of a permanent settlement, and finally, despite the threat of war with Spain, Queen Elizabeth I had consented. They crossed the stormy Atlantic, leaving England behind for the promise of a new life. Despite threats of a harsh existence in an unfamiliar wilderness, they came to make a stand on Roanoke Island. And, as their ship anchored in the peaceful waters of Roanoke Sound, the colonists looked landward with a mix of trepidation and anticipation. These brave settlers disappeared into the wilderness, leaving behind no trace of their fate and created a mystery that haunts modern historians as one of America's oldest. **Tradition** says the first Raines in America was among the remnant of the first colony of Virginia carried away by the Croatian Indians among whom were found blue eyed, blond Indians. **Author's Note:** *"No evidence other than tradition exists to support this claim."*

THE 17TH CENTURY

The English colony of Maryland was founded in 1632, by Cecil Colvert, the second Lord Baltimore. Settlers began arriving in 1634. Maryland passed The Religious Tolerance Act, which allowed freedom of religion in America, in 1649. **Francis Raines** arrived in Maryland in **1665**, as part of **"A List of Rebels Transported" from England**. This may mean that he was being sent here because of his religious beliefs, as many Christians were at that time, who refused to join the Church of England. Barbados is an island nation in the West Indies. The first permanent English settlement there began in 1627. Total control of the island was established in 1652. **Robert Raines** arrived in Barbados in **1679**, according to their "Naturalization Records". Jamaica is also an island nation in the West Indies. The English began settling there in 1655 and controlled the island by 1660. **Charles Raines and his wife Mary Raines arrived in Jamaica in 1686** as part of a "List of Emigrants from England to America".

From Early Virginia Immigrants 1623-1666 by Greer:
Ranes Robert, 1655. bu Capt. Thomas Davis, Warwick Co., VA

"Just a Few Steps Ahead of the Holy Axmen of Pope Urban VIII" Listed below are the names of the first Rainey to come to America. The first eight listed were English-born of Sturat Tudor Rainey and his wife, Julia Tudor Brown Rainey. The whole family had been condemned to death by Pope Urban VIII because of the activities of the father against the Roman Church. This family of ten was personally put abord an English ship at Bristol by King Charles I and they sailed away to the English colonies in the New World. Another Son, Virgille Bartholomew Rainey, was born in Connecticut in 1638, making the orginal Rainey family in America number eleven. Listed below are the names of the nine sons, their birth years and where each migrated:

Julius Caesar Rainey	Born 1623	Migrated to Conn. & Mass
Gaius Augustus Rainey	born 1624	migrated to Penn.
Francis Bartholomew Rainey	born 1625	migrated to NC & Tenn

Henry Tudor Rainey	born 1627	migrated to GA & Fla
Claudius Rex Rainey	born 1630	migrated to Miss & LA
Titus Sulla Rainey	born 1631	migrated to Mo & Ark
Charles Stuart Rainey	born 1632	migrated to TX
Agrippa Windsor Rainey	born 1634	migrated to Illinois
Virgil Bartholomew Rainey	born 1638	migrated to Florida

As far as family records show, the edict of death
to all Raineys has never been lifted, either by Pope Urban
VIII or any of his successors.d"   I think the right
spelling for this group shoud be   RANNEY. RAR

THE 18TH CENTURY

Jamestown was the first permanent English settlement in North America in 1608. Virginia became a royal colony in 1624. In **1723, another Robert Raines** arrived here, according to a resource entitled "Cavaliers & Pioneers: Abstracts of Virginia Land". Nova Scotia is one of the four Atlantic Provinces of Canada. It was first explored by Europeans in 1497. Halifax became the first English settlement in 1749. Also, **Richard Raines arrived in Nova Scotia in 1750, according to the "Report: Board of Trustees of Public Affairs".**

THE 19TH CENTURY

Pennsylvania became an English colony in 1681. In 1776, the Declaration of Independence was adopted in the Pennsylvania State House, now called Independence Hall in Philadelphia. John **Raines** arrived in Philadelphia in 1828, according to the "Index of Aliens' Declarations of Intents & Oaths...". California was first settled by Francis Drake in 1479. It became the 31st state to join the United States in 1850. E. Raines arrived in San Francisco in 1856, according to the "San Francisco Genealogical Bulletin". Indiana became the 19th state to join the United States in 1816. Henry **Raines** arrived here (Indiana) in

1861, the same year that the American Civil War began, according to the "Index of Indiana Naturalization Records".

Randolph County, NC, Rains

In Randolph, NC, during the 1770s and 1780s, several Rains men are found in the Randolph County, NC records. Several of them signed petitions in 1785, and there are many land transactions by the Rains family. This Rains family had naming patterns similar to the Rains family in VA, and it is known that they did come from VA. I have found no connection with the Henry Rains, Esquire family, but it is very probable a blood relationship did exist in VA. Perhaps to Henry Rains, the Planter, in Caroline County, VA. However, the Ambrose Rains in Randolph, NC, is not the son of Henry Rains, the Planter, of Caroline County, VA. The Ambrose in Randolph is too young to be him.

Rains in early NC

While NC records prove that **Jeremiah Rains** was in NC by 1704, and may be part of the Henry Rains, Esquire, family, no proof of a connection has been found. **William Rains,** JR., the son of William Rains, came to NC in the 1750s and died in NC. Tradition in the Henry Rains, Esquire, family has a **William Anderson Rains**, 1680, as a possible grandfather to Henry Rains, Esquire. An old silver spoon has been passed down in the Henry Rains, Esquire, family, that is engraved with "William Anderson Rains, 1780," "Oliver Rains, 1765," "John Rains," and "William Rains" in the 1800s.

The fact the William Rains family married into the Goodwin family in VA, and that **John Goodwin Rains** married a Bryan woman in NC, after William Rains had moved to NC from VA, seems to point to a connection. However, no firm proof or facts connect the families. Others say Henry Rains, Esquire, is the son of Henry Rains, of England, and Esther Chapman. Again, I believe that to be conjecture, with no proof.

The same lack of proven kinship connection holds true for **Gabriel Rains,** who married Ester Ambrose in Wayne County, NC, ca. 1800. I don't know what Rains family Gabriel Rains comes from, or if he is related to Henry Rains, Esquire though one of Henry's sons. This Gabriel Rains was a wealthy man, and was the father of Brigadier General Gabriel James Rains, and Colonel George Washington Rains, who both served in the CSA.

Henry Rains, 1767-1838, the progenitor of the Rains in Bell County, KY, and Claiborne, TN, had no brothers or sisters named "Rains." He only had eight half siblings named **"Lee"** from the marriage of his mother to Captain Thomas Lee, after the death of his father, John Rains, 1742-1772. This is proved by the will of Mary Ingram Rains Lee, and by the lawsuit filed against her estate, in which all her children are named. Henry Rains is listed as her first child. I will start with the first Rains I can prove our family descends from, Henry Rains, Esquire.

Generation No. 1

1. HENRY[2] RAINS, ESQUIRE *(HENRY[1])* was born 1715 in Isle of Wight, VA, and died 1786 in Johnston County, NC. He married ANNE OLIVER 1740 in Johnston County, NC. She was born 1720 in Johnston County, NC, and died 1798 in Johnston County, NC.

Notes for HENRY RAINS, ESQUIRE:
Henry Rains, Esquire, may or may not be the son of Henry Rains of Isle of Wight, VA. It seems obvious that after Henry Rains, Jr. received his inheritance from Henry Rains, Sr., he left the land in VA and moved to NC for a land grant. Henry Rains received his first land grant in Johnston County, NC in 1756. He was interested in politics, and began his career by serving on Juries and serving as a witness to deeds and etc. He took the NC State Public Servants exam. And became an attorney. Henry Rains, Esquire,

appears in the Johnston County, NC court records from 1740 until his death in 1785. Henry Rains, Esquire, served as Sheriff of Johnston County, NC. He also witnessed many deeds and wills. He was a contemporary of John Lee, Esquire, and had several children marry into the John Lee family. Henry Rains served in the Revolutionary War, as a Captain in the Johnston County, NC, Volunteer Militia, under the command of Colonel Needham Bryan. Henry's son Ambrose Rains served as a Lieutenant, and Henry's son Oliver served as an Ensign. Henry Rains, Esquire, was a delegate to the convention of 1777 that ratified the constitution of the United States, and to the convention that wrote the constitution of NC. Henry Rains, Esquire, served several terms in the NC House of Representatives, before and during the Revolutionary War. SEE: NC State Archives, 1775,1776,1777, Raleigh, NC. It is highly probable that Major John Rains, the Tory who served under Colonel David Fanning, was a brother to Captain Henry Rains, but fought for the English King instead of the Colonies. Major John Rains, in command while Colonel Fanning was recuperating from battle wounds, was the man who captured the first non-royal Governor of NC, Governor Burke, and transported him and his entire staff to the British Provost Marshall in Charleston, SC. They were all held as Prisoners of War. This Major John Rains sent the following letter to some of the Colonials in NC: "I do not want you to come into this area spreading your disloyalties against His Majesty, and if you do, I will come and kill you all myself." (NC State Archives, David Fanning Memoirs) Colonel David Fanning, in his personal memoirs, said, "Major John Rains was the first man in NC to take up arms in defense of the Crown." Henry's son John had died in 1772, before the war began, and John's wife, Mary Ingram, had remarried to Captain Thomas Lee and moved to Hawkins County, TN, which was then the Western Reserve Lands of NC. Henry Rains appears in the records of the Johnston County Courts from 1740 until 1780, when he became guardian to his grandson, Henry Rains, son of John Rains and Mary Ingram. Henry Rains received the portion of inheritance that his father would have gotten had he lived.

More About HENRY RAINS, ESQUIRE:
Burial: Johnston County, NC

More About HENRY RAINS and ANNE OLIVER:

Marriage: 1740, Johnston County, NC

Anne Oliver signed as a witness to a deed for William Anderson, in VA ca. 1740. I don't know if it is the same ANNE OLIVER, but it may be. Phoebe and Thomas RAINES were also witnesses to the deed.

Children of HENRY RAINS and ANNE OLIVER are:

2.   i.   JOHN^3 RAINS, b. 1742, Johnston County, NC; d. 1771, Johnston County, NC.

3.   ii.   AMBROSE RAINS, b. 1743, Johnston County, NC; d. 1812, Johnston County, NC.

        iii.   ANNE RAINS, b. 1746, Johnston County, NC; d. 1828, Johnston County, NC; m. LEMUEL LEE.

4.   iv.   OLIVER RAINS, b. 1748, Johnston County, NC; d. 1830, Johnston County, NC.

        v.   ELIZABETH RAINS, b. 1766, Johnston County, NC; d. 1839, Johnston County, NC; m. JAMES LEE; b. 1764, Johnston County, NC; d. 1822, Johnston County, NC.

        vi.   SARAH RAINS, b. 1767; m. (1) ELIAS GEORGE; m. , January 04, 1779; b. Nansemond County, VA. (2) WILLIAM HINNANT, of Johnston County, NC.

More About ELIAS GEORGE and SARAH RAINS:

Marriage: January 04, 1779

Generation No. 2

2. JOHN^3 RAINS *(HENRY^2, HENRY^1)* was born 1742 in Johnston County, NC, and died 1771 in Johnston County, NC, at age 30. He married MARY INGRAM 1765 in Johnston County, NC, daughter of RICHARD INGRAM and ANNE. She was born November 11, 1745 in Johnston County, NC, and died 1823 in Hawkins County, TN. Mary Ingram Rains Lee's will is on file in Hawkins, TN, to be read by anyone interested. John Rains signed the **Regulator Petition** that was sent to the Royal Governor, Lord William Tryon, 'in 1768. He was killed in the Regulator War of 1771. Below is the Johnston Riot Act of 1771, which was passed to destroy the Regulator movement.

John Rains, with only a wife, is found in the 1761 Granville, NC census. John's son Henry Was born in 1767.

NC Regulators-1771

George **RAINES**

1768 signed Regulator advertisement

John RAINES

1768 signed Regulator advertisement (Son of Henry Rains, Esquire)

John **RAINEY**

1768 signed petition to Lord Tryon. DSR Note: This may be John Rains, with an error in some future transcription calling him John "Rainey."

William **RANEY**

1768 signed petition to Tryon, signed Regular advertisement

Johnston Riot Act of 1771

An Act for Preventing Tumultuous and Riotous Assemblies, and for the More Speedy and Effectually Punishing the Rioters, and for Restoring and Preserving the Public Peace of This Province.

Whereas of late many seditious riots and tumults have been in divers parts of this Province to the Disturbance of the Public Peace, the Obstruction of the Courts of Justice, and tending to subvert the Constitution, and the same yet continued and fomented by persons dissatisfied with his Majesty's Government. And whereas it hath been doubted by some how far the Laws now in Force are sufficient to inflict Punishment adequate to such heinous Offenses.

Be it therefore enacted by the Governor, Council and Assembly, and by the Authority of the same, That if any persons, to the number of ten or more, be unlawfully, tumultuously and riotously assembled together, to the disturbance of the public peace, at any time after the first Day of February next, and being openly required or commanded by any one or more justices of the Peace or Sheriff to disperse themselves, and peaceably to depart themselves to their Habitations, shall, to the number of ten or more, notwithstanding such command or request made, remain or continue together by the space of one Hour after such Command or Request, that then continuing together to the number of ten or more, shall be adjudged Felons and shall suffer Death as in Case of Felony, and shall be utterly excluded from his or her clergy, if found guilty by verdict of a jury or shall confess the same, upon his or their arraignment, or will not answer directly to same, according to the Laws of this Province, or shall be mute or shall be outlawed, and in every such justice of the Peace and Sheriff within the limits of their respective jurisdiction, as hereby authorized and empowered, and required on Notice or knowledge of any such unlawful, riotous assembly to resort to the place where such unlawful riots and tumultuous assembly shall be, of Persons to the number of ten or more, and there to make, or cause to be made, such Request or Command.

And be it further enacted by the authority aforesaid, that if such persons so unlawfully, riotously and tumultuously assembled, or ten or more of them, after such request or command made in manner aforesaid, shall continue together and not disperse themselves in one hour, then it shall be lawful to and for every justice of the Peace or Sheriff of the County where such Assembly shall be, and also to and for such Person or Persons as shall be commanded to be aiding and assisting to any such justice of the Peace or Sheriff, who are hereby authorized and empowered and required to command all His Majesty's subjects of this Province of Age and Ability to be assisting to them therein to seize and apprehend such persons so unlawfully, and riotously and tumultuously continuing together after such Request or Command made aforesaid, and forthwith to carry the Persons so apprehended before one or more of His Majesty's Justices of the peace of the County where such persons shall be apprehended in Order to their being proceeded against for such Offenses according to Law. And that if such persons so unlawfully and riotously and tumultuously assembled together, shall happen to be killed, maimed, wounded or hurt in the dispersing, seizing, or appre-hending, or endeavoring to disperse, seize or apprehend them, by rea-son of their resistance, that in every such case, the justice of the Peace, Sheriff, or under sheriff, and all other persons being aiding or assisting to them or any of them, shall be free, discharged and indemnified, as well as the King, his Heirs and Successors, as against all and every other person and Persons of, for and concerning the killing, maiming or hurt-ing any of such person or persons so unlawfully, riotously and tumul-tuously assembled.

And be it further enacted by the Authority aforesaid, that if any Persons to the Number of Ten or more, unlawfully, riotously and tumultuously assembled together to the disturbance of the Public Peace, shall unlaw-fully and with force at any time after the first Day of March next, during the sitting of any of the Courts of Judicature within the Province, and with the intention to obstruct or disturb the Proceedings of such Court, assault, beat or wound or openly threaten to assault, beat or wound any of the judges, Justices or other officers of such Court, during the con-tinuance of the term, or shall assault, beat or wound or openly threaten to assault, beat or wound, shall unlawfully and with Force hinder or obstruct any Sheriff, Coroner, or Collector of the Public Taxes in the discharge or execution of his or their Offices, or shall unlawfully and with force demolish, pull down or destroy any church or Chapel or any building for religious worship or any Court House or Prison, or any Dwelling House, Barn, Stable or other House, that then every such offense shall be adjudged a Felony. And the Offenders therein, their Leaders, Abettors and Advisers, shall be Adjudged felons, and shall suffer death as in due case of Felony, and shall be utterly excluded from his or their clergy; and if found guilty by verdict of a jury, or shall confess the same upon his or their arraignment, or will not answer directly to the same, according to the laws of this Province, or shall stand mute or be outlawed.

And whereas it hath been found by experience that there is great difficulty in bringing to Justice those who have been or may be guilty of any of the offenses before mentioned: for remedy thereof, Be it enacted by the authority aforesaid, that it shall and may be lawful to and for the Attorney-General of this Province for the time being, or his deputies, to commence prosecutions against any person or persons who may have at any time since the first Day of March last, or shall at any time hereafter commit or perpetrate any of the crimes herein before mentioned, in any superior Court within this Province, or in any Court of Oyer and Terminer, by the Governor or Commander-in-Chief for the time being, specially instituted and appointed, and the judges or justices of such Court, are hereby empowered and required to take cognizance of all such crimes and offenses, and proceed to give judgment and award execution thereon, although in a different County or District from that wherein the crime was committed, and that all proceedings thereupon shall be deemed equally valid and sufficient in law as if the same had been prosecuted in the County or District wherein the Offense was committed, any, Law, Usage or Custom to the Contrary notwithstanding.

And be it further enacted, by the authority aforesaid, that the judges or Justices of such Court of Oyer and Terminer so commissioned shall direct the clerk of the District where such Court of Oyer and Terminer is to be held to issue Writs Venire Facias, and the proceedings thereon to be in all respects the same as directed by an act of the Assembly passed at New Bern in January of the year of our Lord, One Thousand seven hundred and sixty-eight, entitled An Act for dividing this Province into six several districts and for establishing a superior Court of Justice in each of the said districts and regulating the proceedings therein, and for providing adequate salaries for the Chief Justices and the associate Justices of the said superior Courts. Provided, nevertheless, that no Person or Persons heretofore guilty of any of the crimes or offenses in this Act before mentioned, altho' convicted thereof in a different County or District from that wherein such Offense was committed, shall be subject to any or other or greater punishment than he or they would or might have been had this Act never been made.

And to the end that the justice of the Province be not eluded by the resistance or escape of such enormous Offenders, Be it further enacted by the authority aforesaid, that from and after the passing of this act, if any Bill or Bills of indictment be found or presented or presentments made against any Person or Persons for any of the crimes or offenses herein before mentioned, it shall and may be lawful for the judges or Justices of the superior Court or Court of Oyer and Terminer, wherein such indictment shall be found or presentment made, and they are hereby empowered and required to issue their proclamation to be affixed or put up at the Court House and each Church or Chapel in the County where the crime was committed, commanding the Person or Persons against whom such bill of indictment is found or presentment made to surrender himself or themselves to the Sheriff of the County wherein such Court is to be held within sixty days. And in case such Person or Persons do not surrender himself or themselves accordingly, he or they shall be deemed guilty of the offense charged in the indictment found or presentment made in manner like as if he or they had been arraigned and convicted thereof by due course of Law; and it shall be lawful to or for any Person or Persons to kill or destroy such Offender or Offenders, and such Person or Persons killing such Offender or Offenders shall be free, discharged and indemnified, as well as against the KING, his heirs and Successors, as against all and every Person or Persons for and concerning the killing and destroying such Offender or Offenders, and the lands and Chattels of such Offender or Offenders shall be forfeited to His Majesty, his Heirs and Successors, to be sold by the Sheriff, for the best price that may be had, at Public venue, after notice by advertisement for ten days, and the Monies arising from such sale to be paid to the Treasurer of the District wherein the same shall be sold, and applied afterwards for defraying the contingent charges of the Government.

And whereas by the great Riots and insurrections at the last superior Court held for the district of Hillsborough it may be justly apprehended that some endeavors will be made to punish those who have been guilty of such Riots and Insurrections, as well as those who may hereafter be guilty of the crimes and Offenses herein before mentioned: For prevention thereof and restoring Peace and Stability to the Regular Government of this Province, Be it enacted by the Authority aforesaid, that the Governor or Commander-in- Chief for the time being is hereby fully authorized and empowered to order to attend Regiments of Militia in this Province, to be under the command of such Officer or Officers as he may think proper to appoint for that purpose, at the Public Expense, to be by him employed in Aid and Assistance of the execution of this Law, as well as to protect the Sheriffs and Collectors of the Public Revenue in Discharge of their several duties, which draught or Detachments of Officers and Soldiers when made shall be found, provided for, and paid, in the same manner and at the same rates, and subject to the same rules and Discipline as directed in case of insurrection in and by Act of the Assembly made in the year One Thousand seven hundred and sixty-eight, entitled An Act for establishing a Militia in this Province.

And for effectually carrying into execution the purposes aforesaid, Be it further enacted by the authority, aforesaid, that it shall and may be lawful for the Governor and Commander-in-Chief for the time being to, draw upon either or both of the Public Treasurers of this Province, by warrant from under his hand and seal, for the payment of any such sums of Money as shall or may be immediately necessary for the carrying on and performing of such service, and the said Treasurers, or either of them, are hereby directed and required to answer and pay such warrants as aforesaid out of the contingent fund which shall be allowed in their settlement of the public Accounts.

And be it further enacted by the Authority aforesaid, that if any number of men shall be found embodied and in an armed and hostile manner, to withstand or oppose any Military Forces, raised in Virtue of this Act, and shall, when openly and publicly required, commanded by any justice of the peace or Sheriff of the County where the same shall happen, to lay down their arms and surrender themselves, that then and in such case the said Persons so unlawfully assembled and withstanding, opposing and resisting, shall be considered as traitors, and may be treated accordingly.

And be it further enacted by the Authority aforesaid, that the Justices of every Inferior Court shall cause this Act to be read at the Court House Door, the second Day of each Court for their Counties, and that the Minister, Clerk or Reader of every Parish in this Province shall read or cause to be read at every Church, Chapel or other place of public Worship within their respective parishes, once in every three months at least, immediately after, divine service, during the continuance of this Act.

And be it enacted by the authority aforesaid, that this Act shall continue and be in force for one year, and no longer. Read three times in Open

Assembly and Ratified the 15th Day of January, 1771. WILLIAM TRYON, Governor. JAMES HASSELL, President. RICHARD CASWELL, Speaker. A true Copy of an Act passed last session of the Assembly. ROBERT PALMER, Secretary (Col. Rec. of N. C., Vol. VIII, PP. 481 to 486)

Notes for MARY INGRAM:

Mary Ingram Rains' husband, John Rains, died in 1771, leaving her with a son aged 5. Mary remarried, in 1772, to Captain Thomas Lee, son of John Lee, Esquire. Thomas Lee and Mary moved to Hawkins County, TN. Thomas Lee was appointed Justice of the Peace, by Governor Sevier. Thomas Lee was married three times, and had 14 children. Thomas Lee was guardian to Mary and John Rains' son Henry, until 1780 when Henry Rains, Esquire, his grandfather, and Needham Bryan, Esquire, were appointed guardians for Henry Rains, son of John Rains and Mary Ingram Rains Lee. SEE: Johnston County, NC, court records for 1780. Mary Rains was appointed administrator of her husband John Rains' estate at his death. The two bondsmen were her brother-in-law, Oliver Rains, and her father, Richard Ingram. SEE: Johnston County, NC court records for 1773. NOTE: In the will of her father, Richard Ingram, probated February term of Johnston County Court, Richard left his daughter two Negro slaves named "Pen" and "Caleb."

The will of John Lee, Esquire, of Johnston, NC, is hereby offered as **proof of Thomas Lee being the son of John Lee, Esquire: Johnston County, NC—Wills—John Lee, Sr.—1766**

Will of John Lee, Sr., Johnston County, NC
Written December 4, 1766
Proved February Court 1768

Wife: **Mary Lee**—"this plantation whereon I now live and all my personal estate during her life or widowhood."

Son: **Robert Lee**—Negro boy, Seasser (Caesar)

Son: **Edward Lee**—100 a. in low grounds of Neuse River whereon
he has cleared a plantation adjoining John Lee's line.
100 a. in low grounds called John Green's field.
75 a. on Mill Creek at the bridge, and one negro
boy, Abel

Son: **John Lee**—200 a. in low grounds of the river whereon is
a plantation called Cows Bones. 100 a. in Bearhill
adjoining his own land. Two negroes: boy, Charles;
girl, Linn

Son: **Thomas Lee**—after wife's decease or widowhood, plantation
"whereon I now live with remaining part of the low
grounds." 200 a. in the low grounds called "fredricks
lands" and "part of a tract of land called Trapnals
lands being part joyning the plantation it being
divided by a line of marked trees beginning at a
hickory tree at the mouth of Cypros gut on the river
and running by the line of marked trees to the back
line." Negro man, Cuggo; negro girl, Jenney

Son: **Fredrick Lee**—negro wench, Rachel

Dau: **___ Powell**—see end of file
Dau: **Mary Ballanger**—negro wench, Nice, and remaining part of
Trapnals lands

Dau: **Sabray Green**—negro girl, Bine, and 20 pounds prock to be
paid out of estate

Grandson: **Shadrack Ingram**—one plantation of 200 a. adjoining
Richard Ingram's and John Lee's line. 300 a. on White
Oak Swamp, a branch of Mill Creek. Negro girl, Judah

Remainder of estate, after wife's decease or widowhood, to be equally divided "amongst my children above named."

Executors: sons, Edward Lee and John Lee
Witnesses: Ricard "x" Dees, Gilbird "x" hix, Saml. Smith, Jr.

John (his mark) Lee

Inferior Court of Pleas and Quarter Sessions: "The Last Will and testament of John Lee was in Open Court provd by the Oath of Gilberd Hix, and Samuel Smith, Jr. where upon the Exor. therein named, to wit, Edwd. Lee and John Lee, came into Court and took the oath of executor."
   (Johnston Co., NC County Court Minutes, 1767 through 1777,
   Book II, #38, p. 17. By: Weynette Parks Haun)

RE: Dau.: ___ Powell. The item between the bequest to son, Fredrick, and bequest to daughter, Mary Ballanger, has been partially obliterated due to a fold in the will. Fairly legible are the words: "Item __ Pow ___ ___ one negro wench called ___ and her child called Bristor to her and her heirs forever." Mr. George Stephenson of the NC Archives revealed that the last name of the daughter was **Powell**.

Re: Thomas Lee. Thomas Lee later sold three parcels of the land that John Lee had patented in the name of John Lee.

More About JOHN RAINS and MARY INGRAM:
Marriage: 1765, Johnston County, NC

To prove MARY INGRAM RAINS LEE is daughter of RICHARD INGRAM, I offer the will of RICHARD INGRAM of Johnston County, NC.

RICHARD INGRAM'S WILL 1780

In the name of God Amen—I RICHARD INGRAM of Johnston
County and State of North Carolina being at this time
in a low state of health but of sound mind and memory,
but calling to mind the mortality of body and that it
is appointed for all men once to die do make and
ordain this my last will and testament in manner and
form following that is to say first-princapally.
First of all I recommend my soul into the hands of God
that gave it, as for my body I commit it to the earth
to be buried in a decent manner at the discrestion of
my executors but regarding my worldly estate with
which it hath pleased God to bless me with I dispose
of it in the following manner in the first place I
desire that my just debits and funeral charges be
fully satisified and paid.
I lend to my will beloved wife **ANNIE INGRAM** the
plantation whereon I now live and all my personal
estate for her to be possessed with and enjoy during
her widowhood also four Negros Violet, Rachel, Tan and
Penny also all my stock of horses cattle and hogs all
the above mentioned property.
I give and bequeath unto my son **JOHN INGRAM** seventy
five acres of land more or less whereon he has a
plantation and one Negro girl called Beua and one Negro
boy called Tom to him and his heirs forever.
I give and bequeath unto my son **ABNER INGRAM** one Negro
boy called Toney also the first young negro that is
raised and if there is never one raised the value of
one made out of my stock after my wifes enjoyment has
expired to him and his heirs forever.

I give and bequeath to my son **WILLIAM INGRAM** two
hundred acres of land whereon he has improvements and
seventy five acres of land whereon I now live with all
my improvements thereon and one negro boy called
Boston and one negro wench called Violet to him and
his heirs forever.
I give and bequeath unto my daughter **PHERIBY LEE** two
negros Nell & Fillis to her and her heirs forever.
I give and bequeath to my daughter **MARY LEE** two negros
a boy and a girl Pen and Colo(p or s?) to her and her
heirs forever.
I give and bequeath to my daughter **ZILPHIA AVERA** two
negros called Tena and Rachel to her and her heirs
forever.
I will that the remaining part of my estate after my
wifes widowhood be equally divided amongst my children
above named to be equally divided by my executors here
after named and I do hereby appoint my son **JOHN INGRAM**
and **WILLIAM INGRAM** to be my whole and sole executors
of this my last will and testament either by revoking
and disannulling all other and former wills and
testaments by me before made. In witness whereof I
have hereunto set hand and affixed my seal this the
5th day of December in the year of our Lord **One
Thousand Seven Hundred and Eighty. (1780)**

Test. Rich(His mark) Ingram Seal
Will A (cut off when copied) **Author's Note:** Spelling errors are left as they were in
the will. Mry Ingram is married to Thomas Lee by the time her father died.

CHAPTER 4

John Rains in Johnston County, North Carolina

Child of JOHN RAINS and MARY INGRAM is:

5.   i.   HENRY[4] RAINS, b. 1767, Johnston County, NC; d. 1838, Knox County, KY.

3. AMBROSE[3] RAINS *(HENRY[2], HENRY[1])* was born 1743 in Johnston County, NC, and died 1812 in Johnston County, NC. He married CHRISTIANA in Johnston County, NC. She was born 1745 in Johnston County, NC, and died 1830 in Johnston County, NC.

More About AMBROSE RAINS and CHRISTIANA:
Marriage: Johnston County, NC

Children of AMBROSE RAINS and CHRISTIANA are:

    i.   JOHN[4] RAINS, b. 1760.

    ii.   EDNA RAINS, b. 1765.

    iii.   HENRY RAINS, b. 1772.

    iv.   ANN RAINS, b. 1774.

    v.   ELIZABETH RAINS, b. 1795, Johnston County, NC. Married PHILLIP RAIFORD, Esquire, 1823.

6.   v.   AMBROSE BETHEA RAINS, b. 1799, Johnston County, NC; d. February 22, 1860, Crawford County, Ill.

4. OLIVER[3] RAINS (*HENRY[2], HENRY[1]*) was born 1748 in Johnston County, NC, and died 1830 in Johnston County, NC. He married MARY RAIFORD 1771 in Johnston County, NC. She was born 1750 in Johnston County, NC, and died 1840 in Johnston County, NC.

More About OLIVER RAINS and MARY RAIFORD:
Marriage: 1771, Johnston County, NC

Children of OLIVER RAINS and MARY RAIFORD are:
    i.   JOHN[4] RAINS, b. 1772.
    ii.   ELEANOR RAINS, b. 1774.
    iii.   OLIVER RAINS, b. 1775.
    iv.   CORDELIA RAINS, b. 1777.
    v.   HENRY RAINS, b. 1778.
    vi.   MARY RAINS, b. 1780.

Generation No. 3

5. HENRY[4] RAINS (*JOHN[3], HENRY[2], HENRY[1]*) was born 1767 in Johnston County, NC, and died 1838 in Knox County, KY. He married MARTHA PATSY LANE 1790 in Hawkins County, TN. She was born 1777 in Wise County, VA, and died 1854 in Knox County, KY.

CHAPTER 5

Henry Rains in Tennessee and Kentucky

Notes for HENRY RAINS:

Henry Rains inherited many acres of land in Johnston County, NC, from his grandfather, Henry Rains, Esquire. **SEE:** Henry Rains, Esquire, land division, a separate page at end of document. After his father, John Rains died in 1771, Henry's mother Mary Ingram, remarried to Captain Thomas Lee, as his third wife. Thomas Lee was appointed guardian for Henry in the November 1774 term of Johnston County, NC court. He relinquished the guardianship to Henry Rains, Esquire, and Colonel Needham Bryan, in May, 1780. Henry sold most of the land he inherited from his grandfather, Henry Rains, Esquire, to his uncle Ambrose Rains, before relocating from Hawkins County, TN to Knox County, KY. Henry Rains served in the Hawkins County, TN, Militia in Captain John Blair's Company of Militia Horsemen in 1788, as a private, fighting the Chickamauga Indians. **SEE:** Captain John Blair's pay roll, October 9, 1792, verified by James White, Justice of the Peace, and approved by Brig. Gen. Joseph Martin, of the District of Washington, NC. This info. from a page copyrighted by Jackie Robinson, and posted on the TN Genweb, Hawkins County, TN site. His stepbrother Thomas Lee, Jr., and his half-brothers Micajah Lee, and Hopkins Lee served with him, all as privates. Henry Rains served in the War of 1812 as a Captain in the KY Volunteers. **SEE:** KY War of 1812 records. After his mother Mary Ingram Rains Lee died, Henry

Rains is listed as her first heir, along with Needham Lee, John Lee, Winiford Bailey, Zilpha Bailey, (Thomas Bailey's wife) William Lee, Edward Lee, James Lee and Mary Griffin. (wife of Jones Griffin) SEE: The suit filed in chancery to divide the estate of Mary Ingram Lee, 1822, Hawkins County, TN. That suit names Henry Rains as Mary's first child. Henry was half brother to all the others listed. "John Lee, Esquire of Johnston County, NC and some of his descendants" by Weldon Johnston et al…page 56. AND "Some of the descendants of Captain Thomas Lee of Hawkins County, TN," written by Weldon Johnston…page 2. Henry Rains died intestate, and his widow applied for and received, in Knox Circuit Court in 1837, her "dower rights." She also applied for her husband's pension benefits for his War of 1812 service in 1837. This indicates that Henry died in 1837. Henry appears in the Knox County, KY court records in 1837, so he was certainly alive then. Henry actually died in 1838. Henry is shown on the list of voters for Hawkins County, TN, for March 8, 1790, held to elect a Representative to Congress, for the western district of North Carolina. TN was part of NC at that time. Candidates were William Coke, John Sevier and John Rhea, Esquire. The election was certified by Thomas Amis, JP. Henry Rains saw the Powell Valley and Yellow Creek Valley during his service in 1788, against the Chicamauga Indians. He apparently liked what he saw, and came back to settle there in 1796 or 1797. His property is shown on a map of 1797 as "the Henry Rains Plantation." Next door to Henry is "the William Lane Plantation." Since Henry named his first son "John" after his own father, and named his second son "William" as was customary in those days, after the wife's father, and then named his last son "Henry Lane Rains" the connection to the William Lane family is clear. Henry Rains daughter, Sarah Rains, who married James Kellems, named her first son "Henry Lane Kellems." Henry Rains bought land grants from Elisha Wallin, in 1813, in Knox County, KY, called "Tellico Grant # 485, consisting of 200 acres, as assignee of Elisha Wallin." Henry Rains also had four land grants in MO, one from President John Quincy Adams, dated 1820, and three from President Andrew Jackson, dated 1833 and 1836. Henry had land deeds in Knox and Harlan Counties, KY. Henry was in KY before 1802, and was counted in 1802.

HARLAN COUNTY, KY DEEDS 1826

Wm. TINSLEY Sr. and wife Polly to Henry RAINES Apr. 1, 1826 for $600., 100 acres, 1/2 of a 200 acre survey entered on Yellow Creek to Elisha WALLEN & **pat. Aug. 6, 1818 to said Raines**, on the N. bank of the Stoney Fk. Wit: Robt. GEORGE, **John TURNER & Preston DAVIS.**

Knox & Harlan Deeds with Rains, Davis and Turner

Edward BEATY & wife Nancy of Lee Co VA to George HOSKINS 17 Aug 1821 for $300—Land on Brownies Creek Witnesses: Milton EVE, Rheuben MOSS, William BEATY, William HEISKILL, James BRIT-TAIN, David HOGAN and John RAINES (deed recorded clerk 19 Sep 1823, dower release recorded 4 March 1824)

James J NOWILL of Claibourn (sic) Co TN to Israel MINIARD of Clay County 19 Apr 1824 for $200—150 acres on big Yellow Creek Witnesses: John & William TURNER and Samuel MATHIS

William TINSLEY Sr and wife Polly to Henry RAINES 1 Apr 1826 for $600—100 acres, an equal half of a 200 acre survey on Yellow Creek entered to Elisha WALLEN and patented 6 Aug 1818 to said RAINES located on the north bank of the Stony Fork of said creek Witnesses: Robert GEORGE, John TURNER and Preston DAVIS

> Hugh WHITE of Clay County, Ky, and James WHITE of Washington County, Virginia, to William TINSLEY 8 June 1827 for $600-200 acres on Yellow Creek; mentions William WHITE's line and the "old trace"; crosses the state road Witnesses: Robt GEORGE, Thomas MARCEE, Geo W CRAIG [MARCEE signed by a mark, see next deed]
> page 195/196

Hugh WHITE of Clay County, Ky, and James WHITE of Washington County, Virginia to Richard PIERCE 8 June 1827 for $900-200 acres on Yellow Creek, also crosses state road. Witnesses are the same as the preceding deed but whereas Thomas MARCEE's mark as shown in 194/195 was a plain 'x', here it is a particular mark as sketched. $\mathcal{T}$

Green CLAY and Sally CLAY of Madison County, Kentucky to Robert GEORGE 20 June 1827 "for and in consideration of the sum of one thousand dollars currant money of the United States with interest there on from the 13th day of July 1819"—All right title claim and interest to three tracts on Yellow Creek: 180 acres by patent bearing date of 4 Nov 1806 on the state road just above Four Mile Creek… crosses state road… the narrows below Henry RAINES house"; 340 acres by patent bearing the same date, adjoins third tract, crosses big Yellow Creek… top of the hill above Henry RAINES plantation; 190 acres beginning at corner to the land of Richard DAVIS standing on the Indian line at the foot of black Mingo Mountain, crosses little Yellow Creek. Green and Sally CLAY clearly state that they are not liable for any adverse conflicting claims. Witnesses [in Madison County]: include Brutus G CLAY.

Reuben GIBSON [wife Ara, signed & certified] to Peggy LANE 14 July 1827 for _____—20 acres on little Yellow Creek, part of a 100 acre survey of Carr BRITTAIN's Witnesses: Robert GEORGE & John TURNER

(Is this the Peggy Lane that married Henry Lane Rains?)

Joseph MARCEE and John MARCEE to John TURNER 8 March 1827 for $400—100 acres on Bennetts Fork of Yellow Creek Witnesses: Elisha TINSLEY, Robert GEORGE and Thomas DRAKE.

Jacob SWIGART, Commissioner & Executor of William LITTELL, deceased, and George WALLER by their attorney in fact [see above two instruments] to William SMITH of Rockcastle County, David HOGAN and Henry RAINES, both of Harlan County 1 Jan 1829 for _____—Regarding the Jacob BUCKNER 7000 acre patent, 700 acres to HOGAN including the 200 on which he now lives and the rest on Yellow Creek; 400 to RAINES on Yellow Creek where he now lives and surrounding area; and 1000 to SMITH [patents also held by grantees]

Bell County, KY Deeds & Etc.

May 14, 1883—Ordered by Bell Co. Court to deliver the books to John E. Mason and the books as Justice of the Peace to Robert Partin. Feb. 11, 1884 John C. Partin presented to court an inventory of the estate of Wm. Rains. Allowed $5 for his services as adm. of Wm. Rains estate (May 9, 1887). April 30, 1892, conveyed by deed 100 acres (of land originally surveyed by Elam Partin on June 25, 1866) to James B. Partin for $200.

The division of the land left by Henry Rains, Esquire, in 1786, follows:

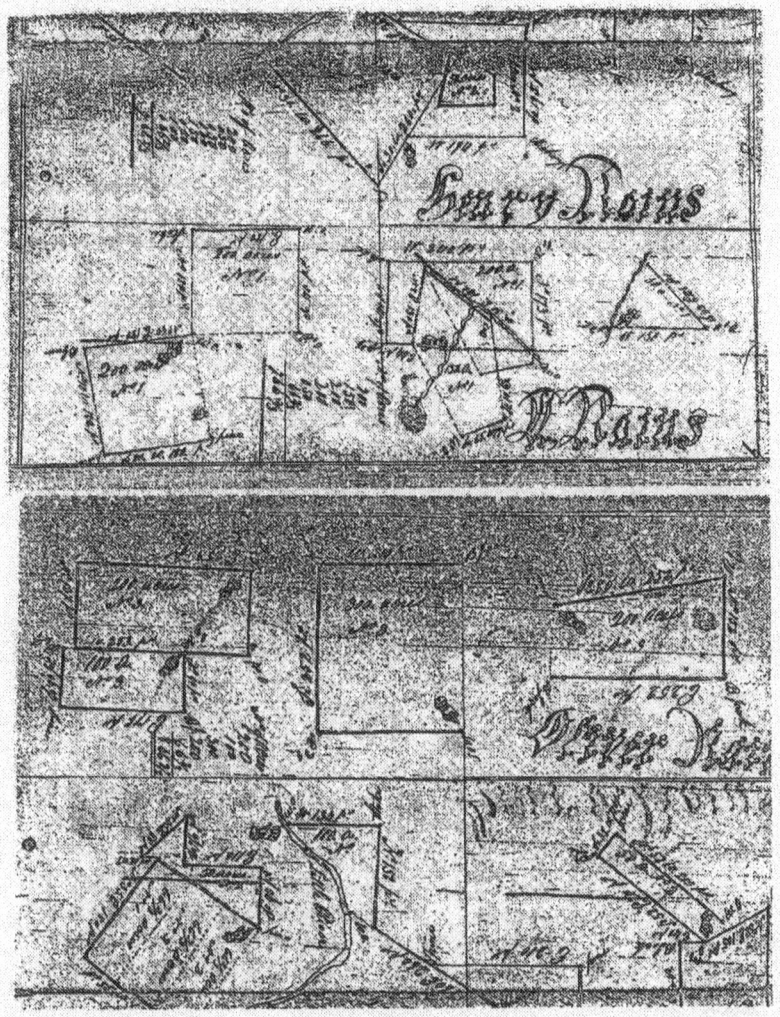

CHAPTER 6

Henry Rains & William Lane

William Lane was in Surry County, VA, in 1782.

1782 Surry County, VA, Census

Frederick Lane	4	6
John Lane	10	6
Lucy Lane	6	-
Micajah Lane	3	1
Thomas Lane	6	4
William Lane	**9**	**4**

William Lane, and John Turner, received land grants in TN in 1780.

1780 TN Land Grants

162. John Turner

163. William Lane

Author's Note: These land grants are for Revolutionary War service, I believe. See record of Craven Regiment below.

Craven Regiment		
Joseph Leech	Colonel	
Richd. Cogdell	Lieut. Colonel	
Thomas Greaves	Major	
Thos. Cl. Howe	Thos Sitgreaves	Osborn Powell
Chris. Neale	Samuel Masters	
John Turner	John Fonville Junr.	Ephraim Lane
Joseph Bryan	John Hill	William Nelson
Arthur Johnston	Bazil Smith	Joseph Hall (moved)
Lewis Bryan	Jacob Johnston	Joseph Bryan Jr.
James Carraway	William Bryan	Thomas Shine
Robert Orme	William Wichliffe	Emanuel Simmons
Frederick Becton	Levin Lane	John Isler
David Lewis	William Speight	Solomon Edwards (dead)
Daniel Shine	Mathew Stevenson	Joseph Kinsey
John Carruthers	David Wharton	Thomas Dalamar

In 1797, William Lane Jr., of Hawkins County, Tn. bought land from William Hall of Sumner County, Tn. This was witnessed by John Lee, William's brother-in-law.

A-154: (blank day and month) 1798, **Benjn. Duncan** to **John Lee**, both Grainger Co. TN, £30, 88? acres on Indian Creek on VA boundary line, line made by Berry to Alexr. Stewart. Wit. **Henry Rains**, Wm. Dougherty. Reg. Nov. 1799. (Henry Rains is half brother to John Lee) (FHL film 968,597)

In 1808, William Lane, Sr., of Knox Co., Kentucky, sold land in Claiborne County Tn., in Powell Valley, including Butcher Springs, to John Lee, his son-in-law. This land was bordered by the Elisha Wallins property. The deed was witnessed by Henry Rains, also Williams's son-in-law, who was living in Knox Co., KY at the time. John Smith and Jacob Pevehouse were also witnesses on the deed. Jacob Pevehouse married Rachel Kellums July 11, 1800, in Grainger Co. Tn., Also at this time, Samuel B. Lane was in Knox County. Sara (Lane) Smith and her husband, Gideon, lived in Knox Co., where it is listed they had a daughter. One should look at the Grainger or Hawkins tax list for the year 1808 to see if a William Lane Jr. was there. That would help to separate the William Lane, Sr., and William Lane, Jr.

Then on 27 October 1819, the above mentioned land was sold to brothers, Elisha and John Wallins. This was of the original tract granted to William Hall from the state of N.Carolina, # 432,22 May 1790. This sounds as if this land was the same land or was connected to the land William Lane of Knox Co. Ky. sold in 1808 that was bordered by Elisha Wallins.

William Lane Jr. was living in Maury Co. at this time. Then in September of 1822, William Lane, still in Maury Co. sells land to Peter Huffacre, who was living in Claiborne. The land was in Claiborne County, and was part of the tract granted to William Hall, by the state of North Carolina. This deed was witnessed by William Hogan and William Davis.

As I look over these deeds, familiar names are listed. It appears that John Lee and William Lane Jr., moved together to Maury Co. Tn. Henry Rains and his wife Martha Patsy, Gideon Smith and wife Sara Lane Smith and Samuel B. Lane moved with William Lane, Sr. to Knox Co. Kentucky.

"If we start to build a family for William Lane Sr., possible children for him would be:"
>
> (in no particular order to age)
>
> Sarah Lane m. Gideon Smith
>
> Frances Lane m. John Lee
>
> Martha Patsy Lane m. Henry Rains
>
> William Lane Jr. m. Winnefred Ingram
>
> Nancy Lane m. David Chadwell
>
> Catherine "Katie" Lane m. William Chadwell
>
> Elizabeth?
>
> Samuel B. Lane m. Sarah (Sally) Asher
>
Note: Lucy Ann Chadwell, d/o of William and Katie (Lane) Chadwell married Henry Lane, s/o Samuel B. Lane.

Contributed by Sandy Spangler. 2001

CHAPTER 7

Henry Rains Knox County, Ky. Census Information

1802 Knox Co Ky tax list 1803, for those counted in 1802

April 8	Allsap, James
April 28	Arthur, John
	Arthur, Joseph
	Arthur, Samuel
	Arthur, Elias
April 30	Anderson, John
May 2	Arnett, Stephen
May 3	Arnett, David
May 13	Allsup, Daniel
May 15	Asher, Dillian
May 18	Arthur, Thomas Sr
	Arthur, Ambrose
	Arthur, Thomas Jr
June 6	Alexander, James
July 4	Allsup, John
July 5	Ayers, Moses

July 6	Aikman, John
July 7	Ayers, Moses Sr
	Ayers, Jacob
April 8	Brown, Moses
	Brown, John
April 28	Bailey, John
	Blanton, Vincent
April 29	Barton, Susannah
	Barton, John
May 3	Brock, Jesse Sr
	Brock, James
	Brock, George
	Brock, Jesse Jr
May 4	Blanton, John
	Blanton, William
	Brittain, James
May 5	Brittain, Parks
May 6	Bailey, Carr
May 12	Brittain, George
May 13	Ballew, Robert
	Bean, George
	Boyd, John
	Ballinger, Richard
May 18	Baker, William
	Baker, Bryson
	Baker, Joseph
May 19	Bagley, Thomas
May 20	Bunch, George
	Brown, James
	Black, David
May 28	Brittain, Levi

June 6	Boyd, Robert
June 7	Brindlee, Stephen
	Ball, Joseph
June 9	(Brewton), Jacob
June 10	Blake, John
	Blake, Willoughby
June 14	Blakely, Robert
	Blakely, Curtis
	Brummet, William
	Brummet, Pierson
	Bryant, James
	Brummet, James
June 15	Brindlee, Robert
July 1	Bracket, John
July 4	Barber, John
	Berry, Lewis
	Bledsoe, Ezekiel
	Ballinger, Eartham
	Benton, David
	Ballinger, John
	Bailey, James

No BURCH in Knox, KY in 1802 (married into Rains and Turner families)

April 28	Coffee, John
April 30	Coultson, John (COLSON)
	Coultson, James
May 2	Chulmley, John Sr
	Chulmley, John Jr
May 5	Comer, Martin
May 9	Cope, Andrew
May 10	Caldwell, John

May 18	Coultson, Henry
	Cornish, Cyrus
May 20	Carter, Isaac
	Carter, Solomon
June 7	Cox, Frederick
	Cumstalk, Isaac (probably "Comstock")
	Curtis, Nathaniel
	Curtis, Samuel
June 8	Cox, Jesse
	Culton, James
	Canterberry, John
	Cox, Thomas
	Cox, Solomon Sr
	Cox, Christopher
	Cummins, John
June 9	Cox, Nathan
	Cox, Solomon Jr
	Cutbuath, Daniel
	Cutbuath, Benjamin
	Culton, John
June 10	Chaney, Isaac
June 11	Craig, Robert Sr
	Craig, Robert Jr
June 13	Cox, John
	Collet, William
	Cummins, William
	Cummins, Hugh
June 15	Cox, Joseph (A Joseph Cox married a Rains woman in Knox, KY)
	Chisher, William
	Cox, Thomas
	Cox, William
	Cox, Absalom

	Cotterel, John
	Cumstalk, Elizabeth
	Cumstalk, William
	Cumstalk, Joseph
July 4	Canterberry, Zachariah
July 5	Chesnut, John Jr
	Chesnut, Jacob
	Chesnut, William
	Campbell, George
	Campbell, James
July 7	Chesnut, John Sr
	Chesnut, Abraham
July 8	Cane, Peter
	Craig, Andrew
	Craig, George

April 28	Dugger, William
	Davis, John
	Davis, William
	Davis, James
April 29	Daniel, William
	Daniel, Robert
	Daniel, Spencer
	Day, Jesse

Davis, Richard (the Father of Preston Davis, who may have married Margaret Rains)

	Daniel, James
May 13	Dean, John
	Dean, Isaac
May 19	Deweese, Thomas
June 7	Dudley, James

June 8   Dickson, Nathan

June 9   Davenport, Zachariah

June 10 Duncan, Joseph

June 13 Davis, Abner

June 14 Doolan, Abraham

July 4   Deweese, david

July 8   Demoss, Andrew

April 28 Edwards, William

April 29 Engle, Peter

June 6   Eaton, John

June 11 Early, William
         Earley, Joseph

July 4   Elliott, Asahil
         Engle, William

April 8 Ferril, Roger

April 28 Fowler, Isaac

May 3   Fletcher, Ambrose

June 7   Freeman, Aaron
         Fowler, Hellri

June 11 Forguson, Andrew
         Forguson, Thomas

July 5   Farris, Nimrod

July 7   Farris, William
         Farris, John Sr
         Farris, Goerge
         Farris, John Jr

July 8   Farris, Isham
         Farris, John
         Farris, Joseph

April 8 Gordan, Moses

April 2 Gordan, John

April 28 Gibson, Garrett

        Gladdin, Aaron

May 2 Goff, John

May 3 Green, Lewis

May 4 Garner, Benjamin

May 18 Goodwin, Thomas

        Goodwin, John

        Goodwin, Joseph

May 19 Grindstaff, Jacob

        Grindstaff, Henry

May 20 Goodwin, Alexander

June 7 Gibson, William

        Ghaston, Hugh

June 9 Gatliff, Reese

        Gatliff, Charles

        Gatliff, Moses

        Gatliff, James

        Gatliff, Cornelius

        Gatliff, Aaron

June 11 Gillis, Joeph Jr

        Gillis, Joseph Sr

July 4 Going, Isaiah

        Going, Claibourn

July 5 Greyham, John

        Goodwin, Henry

        Gillis, William

        Grisham, Uriah

April 27 Horn, Christopher

        Horn, Polley

        Horn, Salley

April 28 Hamlin, Joseph

April 29 Harris, Evan

May 2   Hoskins, Thomas
        Howard, Benjamin
        Howard, Thomas

May 3   Howard, James Sr
        Howard, James Jr
        Hoskins, John Sr
        Hoskins, John Jr

May 4   Hobbs, William
        Harville, John
        Hobbs, Ezekiel
        Hobbs, Christopher

May 6   Harris, John
        Holmes, William
        Howard, William
        Hensley, Washington
        Holloway, William
        Howard, Samuel

May 7   Harris, Matthew

May 9   Harris, Henrietta
        Harris, Polley

May 10 Hensley, Harry
        Hensley, Albert

May 11 Hobbs, Vincent

May 13 Hogan, William
        Hogan, David

May 20 Herndon, Richardson

June 6 Hodges, James

June 9 Hamlin, John

June 11 Hewit, Goldsmith

June 13 Hines, John

June 14 Hudson, David
   Hill, John
June 15 Howith, William
   Hatfield, John
   Hatfield, Joseph
July 8 Hail, James

April 28 Ingrum, Ebenezer
June 6 Ivy, Wilson

April 28 Johnson, Joseph Sr
   Johnson, Joseph Jr
May 2 Jones, Thomas
May 3 Jackson, James
   Jackson, Garrett
May 5 Jones, Edmund
May 6 Jones, John
   Jones, Stephen
   Jones, Elijah
   Jones, Wayman
June 6 Johnson, Thomas
   Johnson, James
June 13 Johnson, William
July 4 Johnson, David
July 5 Johnson, David

May 2 **Kellums, Gilbert** (is this really "John Gilbert Kellems?)
May 6 Keggings, John
May 9 Kener, Roadan
June 25 Kennaday, Stephen
   King, Isaac

March 24 Laughlin, John

April 8   **Lain, William** (Father to Martha Patsy Rains and Frances Lane Lee, and Samuel B. Lane)

April 28 Lewis, John

April 30 Laughlin, James

May 3   Lovely, Roze

May 12   Lemaster, Eliasen

         Lemaster, John

         Logan, John

June 7   Logan, William

         Logan, James

         Laughlin, John

June 10 Litton, James

         Litton, Thomas

         Litton, Burton

June 11 Laughlin, Thomas

         Litton, Solomon

July 4   Laughlin, John

April 8   **Massee, Thomas** (this is Reverend Thomas Marsee, who married Nancy Ann Turner)

         Miller, Daniel

April 27 McWherter, Robert

April 28 McClellend, Hugh

         Moore, Jessee

May 2   Miller, Joshua

May 4   Munsey, John

         Munsey, William

May 13   Moore, Thomas

         Moore, William

May 18   Moore, John

         Moore, Isaac

May 19   McWherter, James
May 20   Mahan, James
           Mahan, Anthony
           Miller, David
June 7   Matthews, Samuel
           Mackey, William
           Matthews, David
           Mackey, Benjamin
June 8   Mahan, Hezekiah
           Mahan, Thomas
           McCowen, James
June 9   Millikan, David
           McKee, Matthew
July 4   **Martin, William** (Father of Allison Martin, who married Susannah Rains)
July 5   Meper, John
           McNeal, Jonathan
July 7   (Manifee), William
July 23 Moreland, Absalom

May 4   Nocket, William
May 13   Neail, Arthur
           Nicholson, Joseph
June 6   Newton, Isaac
June 11 Newton, William Jr
           Newton, William Sr

April 28 Oldridge, William
May 4   Osburn, Solomon
           Osburn, Ephraim
May 20   Oneal, Barnabas
June 9   Oaky, Samuek

April 8   Pierce, Richard
April 28   Parks, Moses
April 30   Piercifield, Jeremiah
May 19   Pain, William
             Pain, James
May 20   Parker, Alexander
May 28   Pain, Obadiah
             Pain, Joseph
June 6   Potter, Thomas Jr
             Potter, Richard
             Potter, Thomas Sr
June 7   Pucket, John
             Potter, Thomas
June 9   Petty, William
June 10   Prewet, David Sr
             Prewet, John Jr
June 11   Pemberton, james
June 15   Parker, James
July 4   Pierce, Joseph
July 6   Perril, William
July 7   Prewet, John Sr
             Preet, David Jr

April 9   Rockholds, William
April 27   Raleigh, Joseph
April 28   Rockhold, Charles
May 9   Reed, Robert
             Reed, William
May 10   Robertson, Richard
June 7   Reddick, John
             Reddick, Solomon
             Reddick, Elisha

	Reese, Jahu
	Reese, John
June 8	**Rains, Henry** (this is Henry Rains, 1767-1838)
June 13	Reed, Solomon
June 14	**Rains, Jonathan** (I do not know what relationship, if any, exists between him and Henry Rains)
July 4	Reese, Isaac
July 7	Rhodes, William
July 23	Runnels, Daniel
April 8	Stewart, William
April 27	Sanford, Robert
April 28	Sexon, Isaac
	Sexon, James
	Stephenson, Robert
May 3	Salliers, Isaiah
	Salliers, William
	Sailor, Solomon
May 5	Shackleford, Henry
May 6	Seagraves, Joel
May 7	Spurlock, William
	Smith, Jonathan
May 9	Stewart, Charles
	Smith, Elias
May 10	Smith, David
May 19	Stewart, John Sr
May 20	Sneed, William
May 28	Stewart, John Jr
June 7	Slaughter, John
June 8	Stoe, Joel
	Sears, James
June 10	Stephens, Richard

	Smith, Elijah
	Smith, nathaniel
	Saunders, Henry
June 11	Stotts, James
	Smith, Abraham
June 13	Sears, John
June 14	Smith, Gideon
June 15	Stephenson, Joseph
	Shoemaker, Leonard
July 4	Stewart, Joseph
	Stewart, Alexander
July 6	Sellers, Jonathan
July 7	Sellers, Thomas
July 8	Shotwell, Thomas
	Shotwell, Daniel
July 23	Smith, Jonathan
	Stewart, Charles
	Stewart, Isaac

April 8	**Turner, John** (son of John Turner, Sr., and Mary Cloud)
	Tinsley, William
April 28	**Turner, George**
April 29	Thomas, John Jr
	Thomas, William
May 6	**Turner, William**
June 9	Todd, John
June 11	Thompson, Enoch
June 14	Tie, John
	Tie, George
July 8	Thomas, John Sr
	Taylor. Stephen

June 9   Veach, Amos
          Veach, Charles
June 14   Veach, Elias
          Vannoy, William

April 27 Walker, Renelder
          Walker, Nathaniel
          Walker, Samuel
April 28 White, William
May 2   Williams, Charles
          Wooten, Frederick
May 3   Wilder, Joseph
May 6   Welbourn, Nathan
May 9   Wallace, Richard
          Winkles, James
          Winkles, Jeremiah
          Wadkin, Elisha
May 13   Woodson, Henry
May 18   Walker, John
June 8   White, Reubin
          Wood, Thomas
          Wadkins, Joel
          Wadkins, Jonathan
          Whitecotton, Aaron
          Whitecotton, Goerge
June 14   Wyatt, Thomas
          Wyatt, James
          White, William
June 15   Wallace, John
          Wilson, Michael
July 4   Whitson, Isaac

July 5	Wadkins, Luke
	Woods, John
July 6	Walker, Walter
	(Wade), Isham
	(Wade), Pleasant
July 6	Young, James

CHAPTER 8

Harlan County, KY, deeds with Rains, Turner, Marsee and Lane names.

Hugh WHITE of Clay County, Ky, and James WHITE of Washington County, Virginia, to William TINSLEY 8 June 1827 for $600—200 acres on Yellow Creek; mentions William WHITE's line and the "old trace"; crosses the state road Witnesses: Robt GEORGE, Thomas **MARCEE**, Geo W CRAIG [MARCEE signed by a mark, see next deed]
page 195/196

Hugh WHITE of Clay County, Ky, and James WHITE of Washington County, Virginia to Richard PIERCE 8 June 1827 for $900—200 acres on Yellow Creek, also crosses state road. Witnesses are the same as the preceding deed but whereas Thomas **MARCEE's** mark as shown in 194/195 was a plain 'x', here it is a particular mark as sketched. 𝒯

Green CLAY and Sally CLAY of Madison County, Kentucky to Robert GEORGE 20 June 1827 "for and in consideration of the sum of one thousand dollars currant money of the United States with interest there on from the 13th day of July 1819"—All right title claim and interest to three tracts on Yellow Creek: 180 acres by patent bearing date of 4 Nov 1806 on the state road just above Four Mile Creek... crosses state road... the narrows below Henry **RAINES** house"; 340 acres by patent bearing the same date, adjoins third tract, crosses big Yellow Creek... top of the hill above Henry **RAINES** plantation; 190 acres beginning at corner to the land of Richard **DAVIS** standing on the Indian line at the foot of black Mingo Mountain, crosses little Yellow Creek. Green and Sally CLAY clearly state that they are not liable for any adverse conflicting claims. Witnesses [in Madison County]: include Brutus G CLAY.

Reuben GIBSON [wife Ara, signed & certified] to Peggy **LANE** 14 July 1827 for _____—20 acres on little Yellow Creek, part of a 100 acre survey of Carr BRITTAIN's Witnesses: Robert GEORGE & John **TURNER**

(Is this the Peggy Lane that married Henry Lane Rains?)

Joseph **MARCEE** and John **MARCEE** to John **TURNER** 8 March 1827 for $400—100 acres on Bennetts Fork of Yellow Creek Witnesses: Elisha TINSLEY, Robert GEORGE and Thomas DRAKE.

Jacob SWIGART, Commissioner & Executor of William LITTELL, deceased, and George WALLER by their attorney in fact [see above two instruments] to William SMITH of Rockcastle County, David HOGAN and Henry **RAINES**, both of Harlan County 1 Jan 1829 for _____—Regarding the Jacob BUCKNER 7000 acre patent, 700 acres to HOGAN including the 200 on which he now lives and the rest on Yellow Creek; 400 to **RAINES** on Yellow Creek where he now lives and surrounding area; and 1000 to SMITH [patents also held by grantees] Note: **Henry Rains signed this deed "Henry Rains," not "Raines."**

TN Land Deeds. DSR NOTE: John Lee is half brother to Henry Rains.
A-154: (blank day and month) 1798, **Benjn. Duncan** to **John Lee**, both Grainger Co. TN, £30, 88? acres on Indian Creek on VA boundary line, line made by Berry to Alexr. Stewart. Wit. **Henry Rains**, Wm. Dougherty. Reg. Nov. 1799. (FHL film 968,597)

The suit filed at Martha Rains death, to sell the slaves and divide the estate, names all of Henry Rains children, and the children of his dead children. That suit is listed in Knox County Circuit Court records for 1854, with Dempsey King, son of Mary Rains King, named as commissioner for the court.

CHAPTER 9

Henry Rains Children

More About HENRY RAINS and MARTHA LANE:
Marriage: 1790, Hawkins County, TN

Children of HENRY RAINS and MARTHA LANE are:

7.   i.   SARAH[5] RAINS, b. 1791, Knox County, KY; d. Aft. 1860, Spencer County, IN.
8.   ii.   MARY RAINS, b. 1792, Knox County, KY; d. 1872, Knox County, KY.
9.   iii. MARGARET RAINS, b. 1793, Knox County, KY; d. 1849, Knox County, KY.
10.   iv.   JOHN RAINS, b. 1796, Knox County, KY; d. Aft. 1870, Knox County, KY.
11.   v.   WILLIAM RAINS, b. 1797, Knox County, KY; d. 1889, Bell County, KY.
12.   vi.   NEEDHAM LEE RAINS, b. 1802, Knox County, KY; d. 1849, Knox County, KY.
13.   vii. PATSY RAINS, b. 1802, Knox County, KY; d. 1879, Knox County, KY.
14.   viii. BALLENGER RAINS, b. 1805, Knox County, KY; d. 1859, Knox County, KY.
15.   ix.   HENRY LANE RAINS, b. 1807, Knox County, KY; d. Aft. 1870, Knox County, KY.

6. AMBROSE B.[4] RAINS (*AMBROSE*[3], *HENRY*[2], *HENRY*[1]) was born 1799 in Johnston County, NC, and died February 22, 1860 in Crawford County, Ill. He married (1)

ELIZABETH RICHARDSON. She was born August 17, 1814 in Wayne County, NC, and died September 06, 1873 in Crawford County, Ill. He married (2) MALINDA HILL SACKRIDER. She was born 1817 in Wayne County, NC, and died 1854 in Crawford County, Ill. He married (3) LAVICEY COX BOSWELL. She was born 1817 in Wake County, NC, and died October 28, 1854 in Crawford County, Ill. He married (4) CHARLOTTE COX 1824 in Crawford County, Ill. She was born April 18, 1805 in Wayne County, Ill, and died January 01, 1850 in Crawford County, Ill.

More About AMBROSE RAINS and CHARLOTTE COX:
Marriage: 1824, Crawford County, Ill

Children of AMBROSE RAINS and CHARLOTTE COX are:
    i.   SIMPSON[5] RAINS.
    ii.   LAFAYETTE RAINS.
    iii. HENRY RAINS.

Generation No. 4

7. SARAH[5] RAINS *(HENRY[4], JOHN[3], HENRY[2], HENRY[1])* was born 1791 in Knox County, KY, and died Aft. 1860 in Spencer County, IN. She married JAMES KELLEMS 1811 in Knox County, KY, son of DANIEL KELLEMS and RACHEL. He was born 1786 in Lee County, VA, and died 1842 in Spencer County, IN.

Notes for SARAH RAINS:
Sarah Kellems is named in the lawsuit filed by Speedwell Marsee and Nancy Snuffer Marsee (the daughter of Patsy Rains by her first husband, Preston Snuffer) the granddaughter of Henry Rains and Martha Patsy Lane, as a daughter of Henry and Martha.

Notes for JAMES KELLEMS:
James Kellems was married to Sarah Rains and Catherine Mitchell at the same time. He had children by both women. James Kellems was the first Justice of the Peace in

Indiana, being appointed by the Governor. James Kellems later helped Sarah's nephew John Rains obtain an appointment as Justice of the Peace. James was appointed Squire of Crawford County, In, in 1822 by Governor William Jennings.

More About JAMES KELLEMS and SARAH RAINS:
Marriage: 1811, Knox County, KY

Children of SARAH RAINS and JAMES KELLEMS are:

    i.   HENRY LANE[6] KELLEMS, b. January 08, 1815.

    ii.   MARGARET KELLEMS, b. December 14, 1813.

    iii.   RACHEL KELLEMS, b. November 16, 1818.

    iv.   DANIEL WESLEY KELLEMS, b. November 08, 1819.

    v.   GREEN B. KELLEMS, b. May 15, 1821.

    vi.   JOHN KELLEMS, b. May 07, 1823.

    vii.   NANCY KELLEMS, b. December 16, 1825.

    viii.   SARAH KELLEMS, b. January 22, 1827.

    ix.   SILAS DAVID KELLEMS, b. May 25, 1828.

    x.   JULIANNA KELLEMS, b. July 06, 1830.

    Notes for JULIANNA KELLEMS:
    Julianna Kellems was the daughter of James Kellems and Catherine Mitchell, his second wife whom he kept in a house about a mile from his home with Sarah Rains.

    xi.   JANE KELLEMS, b. October 08, 1831.

    xii.   JAMES KELLEMS, b. November 18, 1831.

    xiii.   WILLIAM M. KELLEMS, b. December 18, 1832.

    xiv.   LUCINDA KELLEMS, b. March 27, 1834.

    xv.   MARTIN C. KELLEMS, b. January 11, 1837.

    xvi.   MARTHA KELLEMS, b. January 26, 1837.

    xvii.   STEWART W. KELLEMS, b. May 07, 1839.

    xviii.   DENNIS KELLEMS, b. September 18, 1842.

8. MARY[5] RAINS *(HENRY[4], JOHN[3], HENRY[2], HENRY[1])* was born 1792 in Knox County, KY, and died 1872 in Knox County, KY. She married SPENCER KING. He was born 1790 in Kentucky, and died Abt. 1849 in Knox County, KY.

Children of MARY RAINS and SPENCER KING are:

	i.	SIDNEY[6] KING, b. 1812.
16.	ii.	MARY "POLLY" KING, b. 1814, Knox County, KY.
	iii.	SPENCER KING, b. 1824.m. EMALINE HAMBLIN. (Spencer KING was born in AL)
	iv.	EMALINE KING, b. 1830.
	v.	WILLIAM D. KING, b. 1842.
	vi.	DEMPSEY KING, b. 1812; m. MARY TURNER.

9. MARGARET[5] RAINS *(HENRY[4], JOHN[3], HENRY[2], HENRY[1])* was born 1793 in Knox County, KY, and died 1849 in Knox County, KY. She married PRESTON? DAVIS. He was born 1800 in Virginia, and died after 1849 in Knox County, KY. **Author's Note:** Preston Davis is named guardian to all Margaret's children. They are all also named in his will as heirs.

Children of MARGARET RAINS and PRESTON? DAVIS are:

	i.	JOHN[6] DAVIS, b. 1830.
	ii.	ELIZABETH DAVIS, b. 1831.
	iii.	HENRY DAVIS, b. 1832.
	iv.	RICHARD DAVIS, b. 1833.
17.	v.	WILLIAM R. DAVIS, b. 1834, Knox County, KY; d. 1900, Bell County, KY.

10. JOHN[5] RAINS *(HENRY[4], JOHN[3], HENRY[2], HENRY[1])* was born 1796 in Knox County, KY, and died Aft. 1870 in Knox County, KY. He married CYNTHIA PEARCY Bef. 1823. She was born 1806 in Knox County, KY, and died Bef. 1850 in Knox County, KY.

More About JOHN RAINS and CYNTHIA PEARCY:
Marriage: Bef. 1823

Children of JOHN RAINS and CYNTHIA PEARCY are:

    i.   SARAH[6] RAINS, b. 1823, Knox County, KY; d. Aft. 1870, Bell County, KY; m. ALLEN HENDERSON, July 24, 1837, Knox County, KY; b. 1816, Knox County, KY; d. Knox County, KY.

        Marriage Notes for SARAH RAINS and ALLEN HENDERSON:
        John Rains witnessed the marriage of his daughter Sarah to Allen Henderson. The marriage was performed by Rev. William A. Evans.

        More About ALLEN HENDERSON and SARAH RAINS:
        Marriage: July 24, 1837, Knox County, KY

18.   ii.   NELSON RAINS, b. 1828, Knox County, KY; d. Knox County, KY.

19.   iii.   POLLY RAINS, b. 1833, Knox County, KY; d. January 17, 1913, Knox County, KY. **Author's Note:** Polly's death certificate, signed by her son Jefferson Rains, lists her mother as "Cynthia." In a lawsuit filed against Green Turner, for Bastardy, the sheriff of Knox County is Dempsey King.

11. WILLIAM[5] RAINS (*HENRY[4], JOHN[3], HENRY[2], HENRY[1]*) was born 1797 in Knox County, KY, and died 1889 in Bell County, KY. He married MARY STEEL. She was born 1802 in Knox County, KY, and 1889.

Children of WILLIAM RAINS and MARY STEEL are:

    i.   JAMES[6] RAINS, b. 1827.

20.   ii.   HENRY S. RAINS, b. 1828, Knox County, KY; d. 1886, Knox County, KY.

    iii.   NANCY RAINS, b. 1830.

    iv.   PEGGY RAINS, b. 1835.

    v.   WILLIAM K. RAINS, b. 1840.

21. vi. ELIZABETH RAINS, b. 1842.

vii. MADISON RAINS, b. 1842; m. THURSEY ELIZABETH ANN RAINS, August 27, 1868; b. 1834.

Notes for THURSEY ELIZABETH ANN RAINS:

Thursy Ann Elizabeth Rains was daughter of Henry Lane Rains and Peggy Lane. In 1873, she and her husband, Madison Rains (son of William Rains and Mary Steel, and her first cousin) sold the interest in the estate she had inherited her grandfather, Samuel B. Lane, Sr., to Henry Lane. She is shown on the 1850 census living in the home of William Lane, who had no daughter named Thursey Ann Elizabeth.

More About MADISON RAINS and THURSEY RAINS:
Marriage: August 27, 1868

viii. PATSY RAINS, b. 1842.

12. NEEDHAM^5 RAINS *(HENRY^4, JOHN^3, HENRY^2, HENRY^1)* was born 1802 in Knox County, KY, and died 1849 in Knox County, KY. He married NANCY TURNER 1828 in Knox County, KY, daughter of JOHN TURNER and ELIZABETH MARSEE. She was born 1807 in Knox County, KY, and died Aft. 1900 in Knox County, KY. I believe Needham was disabled, since he had a male slave caring for him in 1840.

Notes for NANCY TURNER:
Nancy Turner Rains is alive in 1900, and living with her daughter Mary Burch. Mary is 50 years old and married to William Burch, who was born 1848. Nancy Turner Rains lived to be over 95, as did her father John Turner, who lived to be 104 years old.

More About NEEDHAM RAINS and NANCY TURNER:
Marriage: 1828, Knox County, KY

Children of NEEDHAM RAINS and NANCY TURNER are:

  i. LUCINDA[6] RAINS, b. 1833, Knox County, KY; d. Knox County, KY; m. JAMES RAINS, 1865, Knox County, KY; b. Knox County, KY; d. Knox County, KY.

    More About JAMES RAINS and LUCINDA RAINS:
    Marriage: 1865, Knox County, KY

22. ii. ROENNA RAINS, b. 1834, Bell County, KY. Married WILLIAM R. DAVIS, 1854.

23. iii. WILLIAM BALLENGER RAINS, b. 1835, Knox County, KY; d. 1917, Claiborne County, TN.

24. iv. LUCY ANN RAINS, b. July 12, 1839, Knox County, KY; d. February 22, 1924, Lexington, KY.

25. v. ELIZABETH RAINS, b. 1841, Knox County, KY; d. 1909, Knox County, KY.

26. vi. HENRY RAINS, b. 1843, Knox County, KY; d. 1948, Claiborne County, TN.

27. vii. MARY F. RAINS, b. 1849, Knox County, KY; d. Aft. 1900, Knox County, KY.

13. PATSY[5] RAINS (*HENRY*[4], *JOHN*[3], *HENRY*[2], *HENRY*[1]) was born 1802 in Knox County, KY, and died 1879 in Knox County, KY. She married (1) PRESTON SNUFFER 1825 in Knox County, KY. He was born 1798 in Knox County, KY, and died 1832 in Tennessee. She married (2) JOSEPH TURNER 1834, son of JOHN TURNER and ELIZABETH MARSEE. He was born 1800 in Knox County, KY, and died 1880 in Knox County, KY.

Notes for PATSY RAINS:
Patsy Rains first married Preston Snuffer. They had one daughter, Nancy Snuffer. After Preston Snuffer died Patsy Rains married Joseph Turner. Patsy is shown as "Patsy Turner" on the membership rolls of Yellow Creek Baptist Church in 1842.

More About PRESTON SNUFFER and PATSY RAINS:
Marriage: 1825, Knox County, KY

More About JOSEPH TURNER and PATSY RAINS:
Marriage: 1834

Child of PATSY RAINS and PRESTON SNUFFER is:

28.   i.   NANCY[6] SNUFFER, b. December 22, 1826, Knox County, KY; d. December 15, 1911, Garrard County, KY. M. SPEEDWELL MARSEE.

Children of PATSY RAINS and JOSEPH TURNER are:

      ii.   CELIA ANN[6] TURNER, b. 1834, Knox County, KY; m. AARON JONES; b. 1824, Speedwell, Claiborne County, TN.

     iii.   JAMES TURNER, b. 1836.

     iv.   HENRY TURNER, b. 1838.

      v.   TERESA TURNER, b. 1840.

29.   vi.   JOHN TURNER, b. 1842, Knox County, KY. M. ELIZABETH RAINS.

14. BALLENGER[5] RAINS (*HENRY[4], JOHN[3], HENRY[2], HENRY[1]*) was born 1805 in Knox County, KY, and died 1859 in Knox County, KY. He married (1) PEGGY MARSEE. She was born 1807 in Knox County, KY, and died 1856 in Knox County, KY. He married (2) SARAH GREGORY 1857 in Knox County, KY. She was born 1806 in North Carolina, and died 1859 in Knox County, KY.

More About BALLENGER RAINS and SARAH GREGORY:
Marriage: 1857, Knox County, KY

Children of BALLENGER RAINS and PEGGY MARSEE are:

      i.   SARAH[6] RAINS, b. 1831.

30.   ii.   REDIN RAINS, b. 1832, Knox County, KY; d. Aft. 1880, Knox County, KY.

31.   iii.   JOSIAH S. RAINS, b. 1836, Knox County, KY; d. 1918, Knox County, KY.

     iv.   MARTHA A. RAINS, b. 1843; m. VINSON HAMBLIN, August 27, 1872, Bell County, KY.

Marriage Notes for MARTHA RAINS and VINSON HAMBLIN:
Martha's uncle, Henry Rains, was surety for the marriage bond. Martha's father, Ballenger Rains, died in 1859.

More About VINSON HAMBLIN and MARTHA RAINS:
Marriage: August 27, 1872, Bell County, KY

v. WILLIAM H. RAINS, b. 1844.
vi. GREEN P. RAINS, b. 1847, Knox County, KY; d. Knox County, KY; m. MARTHA RAINS, January 25, 1872, Bell County, KY; b. 1850, Knox County, KY.

More About GREEN RAINS and MARTHA RAINS:
Marriage: January 25, 1872, Bell County, KY

vii. NANCY L. RAINS, b. 1852.
viii. WIKERSON RAINS, b. 1853.
ix. HENRY RAINS, b. 1854.
x. CHARLES RAINS, b. 1855.

15. HENRY LANE[5] RAINS *(HENRY[4], JOHN[3], HENRY[2], HENRY[1])* was born 1807 in Knox County, KY, and died Aft. 1870 in Knox County, KY. He married (1) PEGGY LAYNE. She was born 1812 in Claiborne County, TN. He married (2) MARGARET DENNY January 23, 1848 in Knox County, KY. She was born 1823 in Knox County, KY, and died in Knox County, KY.

Notes for PEGGY LAYNE:
According to the death certificate of Ingram Rains, his mother was Peggy Layne. He and the other children are too old to belong to Margaret Denny, who is only a few years older than Ingram Rains, Susannah Rains, who married Allison Martin, and Thursey Ann Rains.

More About HENRY RAINS and MARGARET DENNY:
Marriage: January 23, 1848, Knox County, KY

Children of HENRY RAINS and MARGARET DENNY are:

  i. INGRAM[6] RAINS, b. February 17, 1832, Knox County, KY; d. April 21, 1915, Bell County, KY; m. (1) SUSAN SMITH; m. (2) JINCY POWELL.

  ii. THURSEY ELIZABETH ANN RAINS, b. 1834; m. MADISON RAINS, August 27, 1868; b. 1842.

Notes for THURSEY ELIZABETH ANN RAINS:
Thursey Ann Elizabeth Rains was daughter of Henry Lane Rains and Margaret Denny. In 1873, she and her husband, Madison Rains (son of William Rains and Mary Steel, and her first cousin) sold the interest in the estate she had inherited from her grandfather, Samuel B. Lane, Sr., to Henry Lane.

More About MADISON RAINS and THURSEY RAINS:
Marriage: August 27, 1868

  iii. SAMUEL RAINS, b. 1836.
32. iv. JOHN C. RAINS, b. 1839, Knox County, KY; d. Knox County, KY.
33. v. SUSAN RAINS, b. 1830, Knox County, KY; d. Aft. 1870. Married ALLISON MARTIN

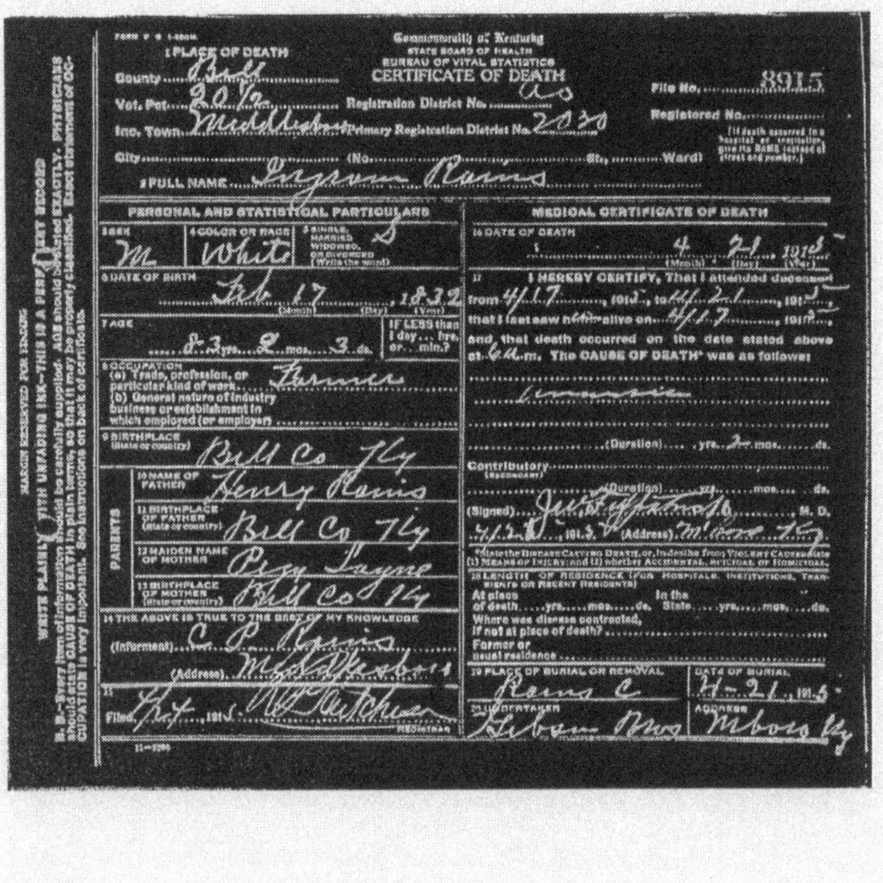

Commonwealth of Kentucky
STATE BOARD OF HEALTH
BUREAU OF VITAL STATISTICS
CERTIFICATE OF DEATH

1 PLACE OF DEATH
County Bell
Vot. Pct. 20 ½ Registration District No.
Inc. Town Middlesboro Primary Registration District No. 2030
City (No. St., Ward)
File No. 8915
Registered No.
2 FULL NAME Ingram Rains

PERSONAL AND STATISTICAL PARTICULARS

3 SEX M
4 COLOR OR RACE White
5 SINGLE, MARRIED, WIDOWED, OR DIVORCED (Write the word) S
6 DATE OF BIRTH Feb 17, 1832 (Month) (Day) (Year)
7 AGE 83 yrs. 2 mos. 3 ds. IF LESS than 1 day, hrs. or min.?
8 OCCUPATION (a) Trade, profession, or particular kind of work Farmer (b) General nature of industry, business or establishment in which employed (or employer)
9 BIRTHPLACE (State or country) Bell Co Ky
PARENTS
10 NAME OF FATHER Henry Rains
11 BIRTHPLACE OF FATHER (State or country) Bell Co Ky
12 MAIDEN NAME OF MOTHER Peggy Payne
13 BIRTHPLACE OF MOTHER (State or country) Bell Co Ky
14 THE ABOVE IS TRUE TO THE BEST OF MY KNOWLEDGE
(Informant) C. P. Rains
(Address) Middlesboro
15 Filed 4/24, 1915 [illegible] Registrar

MEDICAL CERTIFICATE OF DEATH

16 DATE OF DEATH 4 21 1915 (Month) (Day) (Year)
17 I HEREBY CERTIFY, That I attended deceased from 4/17, 1915, to 4/21, 1915, that I last saw h[illegible] alive on 4/17, 1915, and that death occurred on the date stated above at 6 a.m. The CAUSE OF DEATH was as follows:
Pneumonia
(Duration) yrs. 2 mos. ds.
Contributory (Secondary)
(Duration) yrs. mos. ds.
(Signed) [illegible], M. D.
4/2[illegible], 1915 (Address) M'boro Ky
*State the Disease Causing Death, or, in deaths from Violent Causes, state (1) Means of Injury; and (2) whether Accidental, Suicidal, or Homicidal.
18 LENGTH OF RESIDENCE (For Hospitals, Institutions, Transients or Recent Residents)
At place of death yrs. mos. ds. In the State yrs. mos. ds.
Where was disease contracted, if not at place of death?
Former or usual residence
19 PLACE OF BURIAL OR REMOVAL Rains C
DATE OF BURIAL 4-21, 1915
20 UNDERTAKER Gibson Bros
ADDRESS Mboro Ky

Generation No. 5

16. MARY "POLLY"[6] KING (*MARY*[5] *RAINS, HENRY*[4], *JOHN*[3], *HENRY*[2], *HENRY*[1]) was born 1814 in Knox County, KY. She married THOMAS MARSEE. He was born 1813 in Knox County, KY, and died in Knox County, KY.

Children of MARY KING and THOMAS MARSEE are:

    i.   CHARITY[7] MARSEE, b. December 18, 1854; m. NEEDHAM DAVIS.

    ii.   MARTHA T. MARSEE, b. 1840.

    iii.   SARAH MARSEE, b. 1842.

    iv.   MARY J. MARSEE, b. 1844.

    v.   SIDNEY MARSEE, b. 1845.

    vi.   MARGARET MARSEE, b. 1847.

    vii.   ELIZABETH MARSEE, b. 1849.

17. WILLIAM R.[6] DAVIS (*MARGARET*[5] *RAINS, HENRY*[4], *JOHN*[3], *HENRY*[2], *HENRY*[1]) was born 1834 in Knox County, KY, and died 1900 in Bell County, KY. He married ROENNA RAINS 1854 in Knox County, KY, daughter of NEEDHAM RAINS and NANCY TURNER. She was born 1834 in Bell County, KY.

More About WILLIAM DAVIS and ROENNA RAINS:
Marriage: 1854, Knox County, KY

Children of WILLIAM DAVIS and ROENNA RAINS are:

    i.   JOHN[7] DAVIS, b. 1858.

    ii.   ELIZABETH DAVIS, b. 1860.

    iii.   WILLIAM DAVIS, b. 1862.

    iv.   NEEDHAM DAVIS, b. March 01, 1863, Knox County, KY; d. January 01, 1927, Bell County, KY; m. CHARITY MARSEE, 1884; b. 1867, Knox County, KY; d. Bell County, KY.

v.   ALICE DAVIS, B. 1865. Married HENDRICKSON.

More About NEEDHAM DAVIS and CHARITY MARSEE:
Marriage: 1884

18. NELSON[6] RAINS *(JOHN[5], HENRY[4], JOHN[3], HENRY[2], HENRY[1])* was born 1828 in Knox County, KY, and died in Knox County, KY. He married MARY MARSEE. She was born 1829 in Knox County, KY, and died in Knox County, KY.

Children of NELSON RAINS and MARY MARSEE are:

i.   JANE[7] RAINS, b. 1851, Knox County, KY; d. Knox County, KY; m. WILLIAM TURNER, October 01, 1869; b. 1848, Knox County, KY; d. Knox County, KY.

More About WILLIAM TURNER and JANE RAINS:
Marriage: October 01, 1869

ii. SPEEDWELL RAINS, b. 1853, Knox County, KY; d. Knox County, KY; m. FANNIE MARSEE, February 26, 1878; b. 1856, Knox County, KY; d. Knox County, KY.

More About SPEEDWELL RAINS and FANNIE MARSEE:
Marriage: February 26, 1878

iii. SARAH RAINS, b. 1855.
iv. FRANCES RAINS, b. 1859.

19. POLLY[6] RAINS *(JOHN[5], HENRY[4], JOHN[3], HENRY[2], HENRY[1])* was born 1833 in Knox County, KY, and died January 17, 1913 in Knox County, KY. She had a son by HENRY FORTNER , according to birth records, but never married him.

Notes for POLLY RAINS:

Polly's death certificate lists her parents as John Rains and Cynthia Rains. The only Cynthia who married a John Rains was Cynthia Pearcy. Polly is listed in the Knox County Court books as suing Green Turner for Bastardy and refusing to marry her. (Knox County Court, Order book L, page 310) Polly Had one son by Henry Fortner out of wedlock, and I have never found any marriage record for her.

FORM V S 1 900M   2-29-12

Commonwealth of Kentucky
STATE BOARD OF HEALTH
BUREAU OF VITAL STATISTICS
1 PLACE OF DEATH

CERTIFICATE OF DEATH

File No. **445**

County ...... *Bell*

Vet. Dis. *Greasy Creek* No. *14* Registration District No. *5-126*

Registered No. *1*

[If death occurred in a hospital or institution give its NAME instead of street and number.]

Inc. Town .... Primary Registration District No. *5-126*

City *BellJellico P.O.* ...(No. .... St., ... Ward)

2 FULL NAME ...... *Polly Rains*

PERSONAL AND STATISTICAL PARTICULARS

3 SEX	4 COLOR OR RACE	5 SINGLE MARRIED, WIDOWED OR DIVORCED (Write the word)
Female	*White*	*Single*

6 DATE OF BIRTH *1833*
(Month) (Day) (Year)

7 AGE *8.0* yrs. ...... mos. ...... ds.

IF LESS than 1 day .., hrs. or ...min.?

8 OCCUPATION
(a) Trade, profession, or particular kind of work. *None*
(b) General nature of industry business or establishment in which employed (or employer)

9 BIRTHPLACE (State or country) *Kentucky*

10 NAME OF FATHER *John Rains*

11 BIRTHPLACE OF FATHER (State or country) *Kentucky*

12 MAIDEN NAME OF MOTHER *Cyntha Rains*

13 BIRTHPLACE OF MOTHER (State or country) *Kentucky*

14 THE ABOVE IS TRUE TO THE BEST OF MY KNOWLEDGE

(Informant) *J. Jeff... Rains*

(Address) *Artemus. Ky*

15 Filed *Jan. 20, 1913 Daniel Mc. Golf...* REGISTRAR

11-7161

MEDICAL CERTIFICATE OF DEATH

16 DATE OF DEATH *1 17 1913*
(Month) (Day) (Year)

17 HEREBY CERTIFY, That I attended deceased
from *Dec. 25, 1912,* to *Jan 17, 1913*
that I last saw her alive on *Jan. 17, 1913*
and that death occurred on the date stated above
at *8* m. The CAUSE OF DEATH was as follows:
Influenza and
O.p. Age

.... (Duration) ..... yrs. ..... mos. *2 K.* ds.

Contributory
(SECONDARY)
.... (Duration) ..... yrs. ..... mos. ..... ds.

(Signed) *G.T. Carum* M. D.

Jan. 18, 1913 (Address) *BellJellico. Ky.*

State the DISEASE CAUSING DEATH, or, in deaths from VIOLENT CAUSES state (1) MEANS OF INJURY; and (2) whether ACCIDENTAL, SUICIDAL, or HOMICIDAL.

18 LENGTH OF RESIDENCE (For Hospitals, Institutions, Transients or Recent Residents)
At place ...yrs. ...mos. ...ds. In the
of death ...yrs. ...mos. ...ds. State ...yrs. ...mos. ...ds.
Where was disease contracted, if not at place of death? ....
Former or usual residence ....

19 PLACE OF BURIAL OR REMOVAL	DATE OF BURIAL
W.H. King Grave Yard	*Jan. 18, 1913*

UNDERTAKER   ADDRESS
Jeff. Rains Artemus Ky

More About HENRY FORTNER and POLLY RAINS:
Single: Never married

Children of POLLY RAINS and HENRY FORTNER are:

    i.   JEFFERSON[7] RAINS, b. April 15, 1853.

    ii.   SIDNEY ANN RAINS, b. 1859; m. JOHN RUFUS SOWDERS, 1884; b. May 22, 1859, Knox County, KY.

        More About JOHN SOWDERS and SIDNEY RAINS:
        Marriage: 1884

20. HENRY S.[6] RAINS (*WILLIAM[5]*, *HENRY[4]*, *JOHN[3]*, *HENRY[2]*, *HENRY[1]*) was born 1828 in Knox County, KY, and died 1886 in Knox County, KY. He married MARGARET TURNER August 15, 1859 in Knox County, KY. She was born 1833 in Knox County, KY, and died Aft. 1880 in Knox County, KY.

Marriage Notes for HENRY RAINS and MARGARET TURNER:
Witnesses were Thomas Marsee and Robert Turner. Minister was Hezikiah Godwin.

More About HENRY RAINS and MARGARET TURNER:
Marriage: August 15, 1859, Knox County, KY

Children of HENRY RAINS and MARGARET TURNER are:

34.   i.   WILLIAM A.[7] RAINS, b. 1861, Knox County, KY; d. June 03, 1920, Bell County, KY.

    ii.   JAMES M. RAINS, b. 1863.

    iii. MARY E. RAINS, b. 1866.

    iv. HENRY M. RAINS, b. 1869.

    v.   GRAY RAINS, b. October 1874.

21. ELIZABETH[6] RAINS *(WILLIAM[5], HENRY[4], JOHN[3], HENRY[2], HENRY[1])* was born 1842. She married JOHN TURNER January 30, 1867 in Joseph Turner's house, son of JOSEPH TURNER and PATSY RAINS. He was born 1842 in Knox County, KY.

Marriage Notes for ELIZABETH RAINS and JOHN TURNER:
James Turner, William R. Davis and Henry S. Rains witnessed the marriage.

More About JOHN TURNER and ELIZABETH RAINS:
Marriage: January 30, 1867, Joseph Turner's house

Children of ELIZABETH RAINS and JOHN TURNER are:

	i.	JANE ANN[7] TURNER, b. 1862.
	ii.	AMANDA E. TURNER, b. 1865.
	iii.	JAMES MONROE TURNER, b. May 06, 1874, Bell County, KY; d. January 27, 1949, Bell County, KY; m. ELIZABETH.
	iv.	WILLIAM G. TURNER, b. 1869.
35.	v.	PARALEE TURNER, b. 1872, Bell County, KY.
	vi.	ELIZABETH TURNER, b. 1874.
	vii.	JEFFERSON TURNER, b. 1876.

CHAPTER 10

Rains and Davis Families

22. ROENNA[6] RAINS *(NEEDHAM[5], HENRY[4], JOHN[3], HENRY[2], HENRY[1])* was born 1834 in Bell County, KY. She married WILLIAM R. DAVIS 1854 in Knox County, KY, son of PRESTON DAVIS and MARGARET RAINS. He was born 1834 in Knox County, KY, and died 1900 in Bell County, KY.

More About WILLIAM DAVIS and ROENNA RAINS:
Marriage: 1854, Knox County, KY

Children are listed above under (17) William R. Davis.

23. WILLIAM BALLENGER[6] RAINS *(NEEDHAM[5], HENRY[4], JOHN[3], HENRY[2], HENRY[1])* was born 1835 in Knox County, KY, and died 1917 in Claiborne County, TN. He married SARAH TURNER 1857 in Knox County, KY, daughter of WILLIAM TURNER and MARGARET HOSKINS. She was born 1840 in Knox County, KY, and died 1918 in Claiborne County, TN.

Notes for WILLIAM BALLENGER RAINS:
William B. Rains served in the First KY Volunteers, USA, in the Civil War, as a Captain of Cavalry. From *The History of Bell County, KY*, by FUSON, 1939, interviewing Isaac "Ike" Turner: "After the Civil War, the

most prominent and influential citizen in the Yellow Creek Valley was John C. Colson, who lived in a brick house on the state road. His wife lived to be 90 years old. Colson was a farmer, store-keeper and general all-round leader in things going on. He was post master at one time, and sort of a lawyer. I don't remember that he was ever justice of the peace, though he might have been."

"Billy Rains was also quite a prominent man, and he lived near the Hensley Cemetery. He was the father of Ballinger Rains and Needham Rains." *(this is wrong.* **William Rains was son of Needham Rains, and nephew of Ballenger Rains**) "The post office, which was known as "Yellow Creek," was at the old Jack Mealer place. This place is about where Ned Johnson's home now is, opposite the L & N freight depot."

"It has been said, on good authority, that the Turners, the Rainses, and the Marsees were the first settlers in the Yellow Creek Valley, and that they settled here between 1775-1800. Billy Rains was the first school teacher in the valley, carrying on what was called a private subscription school."

"One of the most talked of things after the war, and before the founding of Middlesborough, was the murder of a man by the name of Wilson by Billy Rains and Will Davis. Rains struck Wilson with a cow bell with a collar on it, and the blow killed him. He was convicted but reprieved." **Author's note:** *William B. Rains was reprieved by the governor and served one night in jail before his release. I think William R. Davis was reprieved at the same time. Isn't it nice to have John Turner as grandfather, since he was so influential in politics? His first cousin, Dempsey King, was Sheriff at the time.*

"This was two or three years before my father died. It was an election fight about two miles down on the state road from Colson's." **Author's note:** *This statement, given by Isaac "Ike" Turner, to Doctor Fuson, is* *backed up by Knox County, KY, court records for 1856. Ike Turner is only wrong about the <u>date of the killing</u>, since it was BEFORE the Civil War, in March 1856. Will Davis is William R. Davis, son of Margaret Rains and Preston? Davis. He is married to William B. Rains' sister, so he and William B. Rains are brothers in law as well as first cousins.*

More About WILLIAM RAINS and SARAH TURNER:
Marriage: 1857, Knox County, KY

Children of WILLIAM RAINS and SARAH TURNER are:

36. i.   FRANKLIN B.[7] RAINS, b. 1858, Knox County, KY; d. August 11, 1940, Bell County, KY.

37. ii.   MILTON LANE RICE RAINS, b. 1863, Knox County, KY; d. Aft. 1900, Bell County, KY.

38. iii. RICHARD RAINS, b. 1866, Knox County, KY; d. 1939, Bell County, KY.

39. iv.   WESLEY C. RAINS, b. 1869, Knox County, KY; d. Aft. 1900, Bell County, KY.

40. v.   PRESTON RAINS, b. 1872, Harlan County, KY; d. 1946, Bell County, KY.

     vi.   JULIA RAINS, b. 1876, Little Clear Creek, Log Mountain, Pineville, Bell County, KY; d. December 27, 1967, Wasioto, Bell County, KY (near Pineville); m. RUEBEN B. EVANS; b. 1872, Little Clear Creek, Log Mountain, Pineville, Bell County, KY; d. January 03, 1944, Wasioto, Bell County, KY (near Pineville).

     vii. JOHN RAINS, b. 1879.

41. viii. HENRY SPEEDWELL RAINS, b. 1881, Knox County, KY; d. 1984, Speedwell, Claiborne County, TN.

     ix.   JOSEPH RAINS, b. 1882, Speedwell, Claiborne County, TN; m. LILLIE GIBSON; b. 1887.

     x.   NICHOLAS RAINS, b. abt. 1882, Claiborne County, TN.

24. LUCY ANN[6] RAINS *(NEEDHAM[5], HENRY[4], JOHN[3], HENRY[2], HENRY[1])* was born July 12, 1839 in Knox County, KY, and died February 22, 1924 in Lexington, KY. She married

THOMAS TURNER June 21, 1857 in Knox County, KY, son of WILLIAM TURNER and MARGARET HOSKINS. He was born August 11, 1836 in Knox County, KY, and died April 25, 1914 in Lexington, KY.

More About THOMAS TURNER and LUCY RAINS:
Marriage: June 21, 1857, Knox County, KY

Children of LUCY RAINS and THOMAS TURNER are:
    i.   GILBERT[7] TURNER, b. 1858.
    ii.   WILLIAM C. TURNER, b. 1862.
    iii. NANCY E. TURNER, b. 1865.
    iv. JAMES H. TURNER, b. 1868.
    v.   LOUISA TURNER, b. 1869.
    vi. LUCY TURNER, b. 1870.
    vii. ROVESTA TURNER, b. 1872.

25. ELIZABETH[6] RAINS *(NEEDHAM[5], HENRY[4], JOHN[3], HENRY[2], HENRY[1])* was born 1841 in Knox County, KY, and died 1909 in Knox County, KY. She married JOSIAH S. RAINS 1861 in Knox County, KY, son of BALLENGER RAINS and PEGGY MARSEE. He was born 1836 in Knox County, KY, and died 1918 in Knox County, KY.

Marriage Notes for ELIZABETH RAINS and JOSIAH RAINS:
Thomas Marsee and Mellisa Marsee Rains, John C. Rains wife, were witnesses. John Colson, Justice of the Peace perfromed the ceremony.

More About JOSIAH RAINS and ELIZABETH RAINS:
Marriage: 1861, Knox County, KY

Children of ELIZABETH RAINS and JOSIAH RAINS are:
    i.   SARENA[7] RAINS, b. 1863.
    ii.   SARMA RAINS, b. 1864.

iii.   WILLIAM RAINS, b. 1865.

iv.   BALLENGER RAINS, b. 1865.

v.   JOHN P. RAINS, b. 1867.

vi.   LOUIS F. RAINS, b. 1870.

vii.   CHARLES RAINS, b. 1872.

viii.   GEORGE T. RAINS, b. 1893.

Notes for GEORGE T. RAINS:

George T. Rains is a grandson of Elizabeth and Josiah Rains.

26. HENRY[6] RAINS *(NEEDHAM[5], HENRY[4], JOHN[3], HENRY[2], HENRY[1])* was born 1843 in Knox County, KY, and died 1948 in Claiborne County, TN. He married SOPHIA ANN HAMLIN MARSEE. She was born 1849 in Knox County, KY, and died in Knox County, KY.

Children of HENRY RAINS and SOPHIA MARSEE are:

i.   SARAH E.[7] RAINS, b. 1870, Bell County, KY; m. B.J. MAIN, JR., August 04, 1892, Bell County, KY; b. 1874, Whitley County, KY.

More About B.J. MAIN and SARAH RAINS:

Marriage: August 04, 1892, Bell County, KY

ii.   NEEDHAM R. RAINS, b. March 17, 1872. m. Nancy Mae Logan.

iii.   MALLISA RAINS, b. 1875.

iv.   JACK R. RAINS, b. 1878.

v.   SIMEON RAINS, b. February 28, 1878.

vi.   MARY A. RAINS, b. 1879.

27. MARY F.[6] RAINS *(NEEDHAM[5], HENRY[4], JOHN[3], HENRY[2], HENRY[1])* was born 1849 in Knox County, KY, and died Aft. 1900 in Knox County, KY. She married WILLIAM

BURCH in Knox County, KY. He was born 1848 in Knox County, KY, and died Aft. 1900 in Knox County, KY.

Notes for MARY F. RAINS:
Mary's mother is living with her in 1900. She is **Nancy Turner Rains**, age 92, widow of Needham Rains.

More About WILLIAM BURCH and MARY RAINS:
Marriage: Knox County, KY

Children of MARY RAINS and WILLIAM BURCH are:

  i. BENJAMIN F.[7] BURCH, b. 1875.
  ii. ROSA A. BURCH, b. 1880.
  iii. CHARLES C. BURCH, b. 1882.
  iv. DAVID T. BURCH, b. 1885.
  v. JOHN S. BURCH, b. 1888.

28. NANCY[6] SNUFFER (*PATSY[5] RAINS, HENRY[4], JOHN[3], HENRY[2], HENRY[1]*) was born December 22, 1826 in Knox County, KY, and died December 15, 1911 in Garrard County, KY. She married SPEEDWELL MARSEE in Knox County, KY. He was born 1826 in Knox County, KY, and died 1906 in Garrard County, KY.

More About SPEEDWELL MARSEE and NANCY SNUFFER:
Marriage: Knox County, KY

Children of NANCY SNUFFER and SPEEDWELL MARSEE are:

  i. JOHN P.[7] MARSEE, b. 1851.
  ii. WILLIAM D. MARSEE, b. 1852.
  iii. FANNY MARSEE, b. 1855.
  iv. JOB MARSEE, b. 1858.
  v. JONAS MARSEE, b. 1860.

vi. NOAH MARSEE, b. 1861.
vii. JOEL MARSEE, b. 1864.

29. JOHN[6] TURNER (*PATSY[5] RAINS, HENRY[4], JOHN[3], HENRY[2], HENRY[1]*) was born 1842 in Knox County, KY. He married ELIZABETH RAINS January 30, 1867 in Joseph Turner's house. Elizabeth a daughter of WILLIAM RAINS and MARY STEEL. She was born 1842.

Marriage Notes for JOHN TURNER and ELIZABETH RAINS:
James Turner, William R. Davis and Henry S. Rains witnessed the marriage.

More About JOHN TURNER and ELIZABETH RAINS:
Marriage: January 30, 1867, Joseph Turner's house

Children are listed above under (21) Elizabeth Rains.

30. REDIN[6] RAINS (*BALLENGER[5], HENRY[4], JOHN[3], HENRY[2], HENRY[1]*) was born 1832 in Knox County, KY, and died Aft. 1880 in Knox County, KY. He married ELIZABETH JONES. She was born 1844 in Knox County, KY, and died Aft. 1880 in Knox County, KY.

Children of REDIN RAINS and ELIZABETH JONES are:
i. MILTON JOEL[7] RAINS, b. 1866.
ii. SARAH RAINS, b. 1867.
iii. MARTHA RAINS, b. 1868, Knox County, KY.
iv. ELIZABETH RAINS, b. 1872.
v. SYNTHIA RAINS, b. 1872.
vi. WILLIAM RAINS, b. 1873.

31. JOSIAH S.[6] RAINS (*BALLENGER[5], HENRY[4], JOHN[3], HENRY[2], HENRY[1]*) was born 1836 in Knox County, KY, and died 1918 in Knox County, KY. He married ELIZABETH RAINS

1861 in Knox County, KY, daughter of NEEDHAM RAINS and NANCY TURNER. She was born 1841 in Knox County, KY, and died 1909 in Knox County, KY.

Marriage Notes for JOSIAH RAINS and ELIZABETH RAINS:
Thomas Marsee and Mellisa Marsee Rains, John C. Rains wife, were witnesses. John Colson, Justice of the Peace performed the ceremony.

More About JOSIAH RAINS and ELIZABETH RAINS:
Marriage: 1861, Knox County, KY

Children are listed above under (25) Elizabeth Rains.

32. JOHN C.[6] RAINS *(HENRY LANE[5], HENRY[4], JOHN[3], HENRY[2], HENRY[1])* was born 1839 in Knox County, KY, and died in Knox County, KY. He married MELLISA MARSEE March 31, 1859 in Knox County, KY. She was born in Knox County, KY.

More About JOHN RAINS and MELLISA MARSEE:
Marriage: March 31, 1859, Knox County, KY
By 1877 John Rains and Mellisa Marsee are divorced. She has remarried to William King, and has two children by him. William King is cousin to John Rains.

Child of JOHN RAINS and MELLISA MARSEE is:
    i.   WILLIAM HENRY[7] RAINS, b. February 21, 1861.
    ii.   FANNIE RAINS, b. 1863.

33. SUSAN[6] RAINS *(HENRY LANE[5], HENRY[4], JOHN[3], HENRY[2], HENRY[1])* was born 1830 in Knox County, KY, and died Aft. 1870. She married ALLISON MARTIN August 25, 1846 in Whitley County, KY, son of WILLIAM MARTIN and ELIZABETH GATLIFF. He was born 1825 in Whitley County, KY.

More About ALLISON MARTIN and SUSAN RAINS:
Marriage: August 25, 1846, Whitley County, KY

Children of SUSAN RAINS and ALLISON MARTIN are:

42.   i.   WILLIAM^7 MARTIN, b. 1859, Whitley County, KY.

      ii.   ELIZABETH MARTIN, b. 1849.

    iii.   MARGARET MARTIN, b. 1851, Whitley County, KY; m. GEORGE MADISON WILLIAMS; b. April 09, 1855, Knox County, KY.

CHAPTER 11

Martin-Gatliff-Rains History

William C. MARTIN b 1786 VA d 3 Jan 1854 Young's Creek, Whitley, KY. He married 10 Jan 1805 Elizabeth (Betsey) GATLIFF (b 11 Dec 1788 Garrard Co., KY d 13 Oct 1856 Whitley Co., KY) They had the following children:

Charles, born 1806 Knox Co., KY. He married Priscilla RAINS
Jane b 1807 KY d TX. She married 23 Sep 1824 Whitley Co., KY to Samuel C. Jones.
Christina b 1808 Knox Co., KY d Nodaway Co., MO. She married 1824 William S. RAINS.
Sarah 'Sally' C. b 29 Oct 1814 Whitley Co., KY d 11 Jan 1865 Whitley Co., KY. She married Joseph HAMBLIN.
Elizabeth b 1815 KY. She married 11 Feb 1842 Campbell Co., TN to Christopher ADKINS.
Peggy b 1818 KY
Joel Marion b 1822 Whitley Co., KY d 26 Jul 1894 Laurel Co., KY. He married #1 1844 Indiana WELLS #2 3 Sep 1848 Mary Anne "Polly" CUMMINS.
Emiliza b 10 Mar 1823 Whitley Co., KY d 13 Mar 1897 Sutton Mills, Whitley, KY. She married 26 Feb 1847 John RAINS.

Louisa b 1824 KY. She married 27 Oct 1842 Campbell Co., TN John Jackson "Jack" RAINS.

Allison b 1825 KY. He married 25 Aug 1846 Whitley Co., KY to **Susannah** RAINS. (This is daughter of Henry Lane Rains & Margaret Lane)

Pleasant b 1827 Whitley Co., KY d 15 Aug 1849 Whitley Co., KY. He married 20 Aug 1847 Whitley Co., KY to Matilda HARRIS.

Mary "Polly" b 1829 KY. She married John Wesley WOODS.

James b 1824 d 20 Aug 1849

Generation No. 6

34. WILLIAM A.[7] RAINS (*HENRY S.*[6], *WILLIAM*[5], *HENRY*[4], *JOHN*[3], *HENRY*[2], *HENRY*[1]) was born 1861 in Knox County, KY, and died June 03, 1920 in Bell County, KY.

Child of WILLIAM A. RAINS is:

    i.   LUTHER DAVID[8] RAINS, m. EMMA YOAKUM.

35. PARALEE[7] TURNER (*JOHN*[6], *PATSY*[5] *RAINS*, *HENRY*[4], *JOHN*[3], *HENRY*[2], *HENRY*[1]) was born 1872 in Bell County, KY. She married (1) GEORGE BLACKBURN June 14, 1891 in Bell County, KY. He was born 1870 in Bell County, KY. She married (2) IRA ROARK 1910 in Bell County, KY.

More About GEORGE BLACKBURN and PARALEE TURNER:
Marriage: June 14, 1891, Bell County, KY

More About IRA ROARK and PARALEE TURNER:
Marriage: 1910, Bell County, KY

Child of PARALEE TURNER and GEORGE BLACKBURN is:

    i.   THOMAS[8] BLACKBURN.

36. FRANKLIN B.[7] RAINS *(WILLIAM BALLENGER[6], NEEDHAM[5], HENRY[4], JOHN[3], HENRY[2], HENRY[1])* was born 1858 in Knox County, KY, and died August 11, 1940 in Bell County, KY. He married FANNIE MARSEE, daughter of WILLIAM MARSEE and KATIE MARSEE. She was born April 04, 1858 in Knox County, KY, and died December 07, 1938 in Bell County, KY.

Children of FRANKLIN RAINS and FANNIE MARSEE are:

    i.   CHARLES[8] RAINS, b. 1896.

    ii.   MINNIE RAINS, b. 1898.

37. MILTON LANE RICE[7] RAINS *(WILLIAM BALLENGER[6], NEEDHAM[5], HENRY[4], JOHN[3], HENRY[2], HENRY[1])* was born 1863 in Knox County, KY, and died Aft. 1900 in Bell County, KY. He married JANE CARTER July 22, 1885 in Knox County, KY, daughter of SOLOMON CARTER and BETTY. She was born 1866 in Knox County, KY, and died Aft. 1900 in Bell County, KY.

More About MILTON RAINS and JANE CARTER:
Marriage: July 22, 1885, Knox County, KY

Children of MILTON RAINS and JANE CARTER are:

    i.   JAMES L.[8] RAINS, b. 1887.

    ii.   MARY A. RAINS, b. 1890.

43.   iii.   WILLIAM RICE RAINS, b. 1892, Bell County, KY; d. Bell County, KY.

    iv.   OSCAR RAINS, b. 1895.

    v.   THOMAS FRANKLIN RAINS, b. 1897, Bell County, KY; d. Bell County, KY; m. JENNY MARSEE, August 06, 1921; b. 1902, Bell County, KY; d. Bell County, KY.

        More About THOMAS RAINS and JENNY MARSEE:
        Marriage: August 06, 1921

    vi.   SALLIE RAINS, b. 1899.

38. RICHARD[7] RAINS (*WILLIAM BALLENGER[6], NEEDHAM[5], HENRY[4], JOHN[3], HENRY[2], HENRY[1]*) was born 1866 in Knox County, KY, and died 1939 in Bell County, KY. He married CORDELIA MARSEE 1896 in Bell County, KY. She was born 1870 in Knox County, KY, and died 1942 in Bell County, KY.

More About RICHARD RAINS and CORDELIA MARSEE:
Marriage: 1896, Bell County, KY

Children of RICHARD RAINS and CORDELIA MARSEE are:

	i.	ELIZABETH[8] RAINS, b. 1897.
	ii.	ADDIE RAINS, b. 1902.
	iii.	JENNIE RAINS, b. 1905.
	iv.	RALPH RAINS, b. 1908.
44.	v.	LUCY RAINS, b. 1911, Bell County, KY; d. 1996, Ohio. Married WILLIAM WILLIAMS SYKES.
	vi.	JACKSON RAINS, b. 1911.

39. WESLEY C.[7] RAINS (*WILLIAM BALLENGER[6], NEEDHAM[5], HENRY[4], JOHN[3], HENRY[2], HENRY[1]*) was born 1869 in Knox County, KY, and died Aft. 1900 in Bell County, KY. He married NILEY MIRACLE in Knox County, KY. She was born 1865 in Knox County, KY, and died Aft. 1900 in Bell County, KY.

Notes for WESLEY C. RAINS:
On a birth certificate application filed in 1942, Stacy Lee Rains says his father's name was "James Wesley Rains." All census records from 1870 forward call him "Wesley C. Rains." His father, William B. Rains, told the census taker in 1870 the names of all his children. Wesley C. Rains was one of them, and was 1 year old. It is possible he changed his name to "James Wesley Rains."

More About WESLEY RAINS and NILEY MIRACLE:
Marriage: Knox County, KY

Children of WESLEY RAINS and NILEY MIRACLE are:

    i.   SALLY[8] RAINS, b. 1902.

   ii.   DEE RAINS, b. 1906.

  iii.   W.P. RAINS, b. 1907.

  iv.   STACEY LEE RAINS, b. 1908.

CHAPTER 12

Preston Rains and Cordelia Turner

40. PRESTON[7] RAINS (*WILLIAM BALLENGER*[6], *NEEDHAM*[5], *HENRY*[4], *JOHN*[3], *HENRY*[2], *HENRY*[1]) was born 1872 in Harlan County, KY, and died 1946 in Bell County, KY. He married (1) CORDELIA TURNER 1896 in ?, daughter of JACKSON TURNER and MARY A.. She was born 1883 in Bell County, KY, and died 1917 in Bell County, KY. He married (2) NANCY SIMPSON 1919.

Notes for PRESTON RAINS:
Preston Rains married Cordelia Turner about 1896. Cordelia died in the influensa pandemic of 1917. Preston Rains married his second wife, Nancy Simpson, in 1919.

More About PRESTON RAINS and CORDELIA TURNER:
Marriage: 1896, ?

More About PRESTON RAINS and NANCY SIMPSON:
Marriage: 1919

Children of PRESTON RAINS and CORDELIA TURNER are:
45.   i.   NILIA MAY[8] RAINS, b. 1899, Bell County, KY; d. Bell County, KY.

	ii.	BERTHA RAINS, b. 1899.
46.	iii.	WILLIAM MCKINLEY RAINS, b. October 12, 1900, Bell County, KY; d. 1985, Bell County, KY.
47.	iv.	EARNEST RAINS, b. 1902, Bell County, KY; d. 1990, Bell County, KY.
48.	v.	JOSHUA RAINS, b. September 14, 1907, Bell County, KY; d. January 12, 1997, Bell County, KY.
49.	vi.	CLARENCE RAINS, b. 1909, Bell County, KY; d. Aft. 1999, Bell County, KY.
50.	vii.	HELEN RAINS, b. 1913, Bell County, KY; d. 1968, Monroe, MI.
51.	viii.	AMANDA RAINS, b. June 15, 1915, Bell County, KY.
52.	ix.	BESSY ELIZABETH RAINS, b. 1920.
	x.	JOSEPH RAINS, b. 1922.

Notes for JOSEPH RAINS:
Joseph is son of Preston Rains and Nancy Simpson.

	xi.	CORDELIA RAINS, b. 1926; m. JOHN BROWNING.
	xii.	EUGENE RAINS, b. 1930.

Notes for EUGENE RAINS:
Eugene Rains is son of Preston Rains and Nancy Simpson.

	xiii.	LILLIAN RAINS, b. 1930.
	xiv.	WALTER RAINS, b. 1931.

Notes for WALTER RAINS:
Walter Rains is son of Preston Rains and Nancy Simpson.

	xv.	OTIS RAINS, b. 1933.

Notes for OTIS RAINS:
Otis Rains is son of Preston Rains and Nancy Simpson.

xvi.   NANCY "NANNIE" RAINS, b. 1934.

Notes for NANNIE RAINS:
Nannie Rains is daughter of Preston Rains and Nancy Simpson.

xvii. JOHN RAINS, b. 1935, Bell County, KY; d. 1935, Bell County, KY.

Notes for JOHN RAINS:
John Rains is son of Preston Rains and Nancy Simpson.

xviii. TWIN BABIES RAINS, b. 1936.

Notes for TWIN BABIES RAINS:
These two children died at birth. They are the children of Preston Rains and Nancy Simpson.

41. HENRY SPEEDWELL[7] RAINS *(WILLIAM BALLENGER[6], NEEDHAM[5], HENRY[4], JOHN[3], HENRY[2], HENRY[1])* was born 1881 in Knox County, KY, and died 1984 in Speedwell, Claiborne County, TN. He married NANCY GIBSON 1904 in Speedwell, Claiborne County, TN. She was born 1883 in Speedwell, Claiborne County, TN.

More About HENRY RAINS and NANCY GIBSON:
Marriage: 1904, Speedwell, Claiborne County, TN

Children of HENRY RAINS and NANCY GIBSON are:
i.   ELGIE[8] RAINS, b. 1907.
ii.   ALBERT (ESTILL) RAINS, b. 1908.
iii.   JOHN RAINS, b. 1911.
iv.   HERMAN RAINS, b. 1912, Speedwell, Claiborne County, TN; d. 1996, Speedwell, Claiborne County, TN; m. MATTIE LEE OWENS, May 27, 1939,

William Mckinley Rains Home, Middlesboro, KY; b. 1915, Speedwell, Claiborne County, TN; d. 1997, Speedwell, Claiborne County, TN.

Marriage Notes for HERMAN RAINS and MATTIE OWENS:
Marriage performed by Herman's first cousin, Rev. William McKinley Rains. Witnesses were W.M. Rains' father, Preston Rains (Herman's uncle) and Leona Sykes, the sister-in-law of William McKinley Rains. The wedding was at the home of William McKinley Rains.

More About HERMAN RAINS and MATTIE OWENS:
Marriage: May 27, 1939, William McKinley Rains Home, Middlesboro, KY

v.   HOBART RAINS, b. 1916.
vi. MARTIN BOYD RAINS, b. 1919.

42. WILLIAM[7] MARTIN *(SUSAN[6] RAINS, HENRY LANE[5], HENRY[4], JOHN[3], HENRY[2], HENRY[1])* was born 1859 in Whitley County, KY. He married RACHEL.

Child of WILLIAM MARTIN and RACHEL is:
i.   ELIJAH[8] MARTIN, b. 1879.

Generation No. 7

43. WILLIAM RICE[8] RAINS *(MILTON LANE RICE[7], WILLIAM BALLENGER[6], NEEDHAM[5], HENRY[4], JOHN[3], HENRY[2], HENRY[1])* was born 1892 in Bell County, KY, and died in Bell County, KY. He married ETHEL ROSE SPROLES January 07, 1917 in Bell County, KY. She was born in Bell County, KY, and died in Bell County, KY.

More About WILLIAM RAINS and ETHEL SPROLES:
Marriage: January 07, 1917, Bell County, KY

Child of WILLIAM RAINS and ETHEL SPROLES is:
53. i. AUDRIE MAE[9] RAINS, b. Bell County, KY.

44. LUCY[8] RAINS *(RICHARD[7], WILLIAM BALLENGER[6], NEEDHAM[5], HENRY[4], JOHN[3], HENRY[2], HENRY[1])* was born 1911 in Bell County, KY, and died 1996 in Ohio. She married WILLIAM SYKES September 24, 1929 in Bell County, KY, son of THOMAS SYKES and MINNIE WHITAKER. He was born 1904 in Bell County, KY, and died 1985 in Ohio.

Notes for WILLIAM SYKES:
William Sykes was the son of Minnie Belle Whitaker and a Mr. Milton Williams. After his mother married Thomas Tidwell Sykes, he took the name "Sykes."

More About WILLIAM SYKES and LUCY RAINS:
Marriage: September 24, 1929, Bell County, KY

Children of LUCY RAINS and WILLIAM SYKES are:
  i. WILLIAM[9] SIKES, b. 1928.
  ii. BETTY JEAN SIKES, b. 1929.

45. NILIA MAY[8] RAINS *(PRESTON[7], WILLIAM BALLENGER[6], NEEDHAM[5], HENRY[4], JOHN[3], HENRY[2], HENRY[1])* was born 1899 in Bell County, KY, and died in Bell County, KY. She married JOHN SIMPSON July 07, 1916 in Bell County, KY. He was born 1890 in Knox County, KY, and died in ?.

More About JOHN SIMPSON and NILIA RAINS:
Marriage: July 07, 1916, Bell County, KY

Children of NILIA RAINS and JOHN SIMPSON are:

    i.   DANIEL[9] SIMPSON.

    ii.   JAMES PRESTON "SHORTY" SIMPSON.

46. WILLIAM MCKINLEY[8] RAINS (*PRESTON[7], WILLIAM BALLENGER[6], NEEDHAM[5], HENRY[4], JOHN[3], HENRY[2], HENRY[1]*) was born October 12, 1900 in Bell County, KY, and died 1985 in Bell County, KY. He married NANCY WHITAKER SYKES October 09, 1920 in Claiborne County, TN, daughter of THOMAS TIDWELL SYKES and MINNIE BELLE WHITAKER. She was born 1909 in Claiborne County, TN, and died 1973 in Bell County, KY.

More About WILLIAM MCKINLEY RAINS:
Burial: 1985, Rains Cemetery, Middlesboro, KY

More About NANCY WHITAKER SYKES:
Burial: 1973, Rains Cemetery, Middlesboro, KY

Marriage Notes for WILLIAM RAINS and NANCY SYKES:
Married by Reverend Brad Lowery

More About WILLIAM RAINS and NANCY SYKES:
Marriage: October 09, 1920, Claiborne County, TN

Name	Rank	State	Unit	Co.	Side	Notes
Rains, Alfred	Pvt	KY	6th Cavalry	M	Union	
Rains, Franklin	Pvt	KY	7th Infantry	G	Union	
Rains, Franklin	Pvt	KY	16th Infantry	F	Union	
Rains, Hiram	Pvt	KY	49th Infantry	G	Union	
Rains, Ingram	Pvt	KY	49th Infantry	K	Union	Son of Henry Lane Rains
Rains, Isam	Pvt	KY	16th Infantry	F	Union	
Rains, James	Pvt	KY	8th Infantry (Consolidated)	E	Union	
Rains, James	Pvt	KY	7th Infantry	G	Union	
Rains, James A.	Pvt	KY	16th Infantry	F	Union	
Rains, John	Pvt	KY	6th Cavalry	E	Union	
Rains, Martin	Pvt	KY	7th Infantry	G	Union	
Rains, Milton G.	Pvt	KY	49th Infantry	G	Union	
Rains, Preston C.	Pvt	KY	49th Infantry	G	Union	
Rains, William B.	Capt	KY	1st Cavalry	B	Union	1836 1917
Rains, William A.	Pvt	KY	3rd Infantry	H	Union	
Rains, Wm. G.	Pvt	KY	1st Cavalry	C	Union	

CHAPTER 13

Rains and Whitaker Families

I thought it would be appropriate to insert my mother's descendency from the **WHITAKER** line.

Nancy Whitaker Sykes descends as follows:

Descendants of William Whitaker

Generation No. 1

1. WILLIAM[1] WHITAKER was born 1695 in Chester County, Pennsylvania, and died 1778 in Rowan County, NC. He married ELIZABETH CARLETON December 13, 1722 in Quaker Meeting House, Chester County, PA. She was born 1700 in Chester County, Pennsylvania, and died 1780 in Rowan County, NC.

More About WILLIAM WHITAKER:
Burial: 1778, Rowan County, NC

More About ELIZABETH CARLETON:
Burial: 1780, Rowan County, NC

More About WILLIAM WHITAKER and ELIZABETH CARLETON:
Marriage: December 13, 1722, Quaker Meeting House, Chester County, PA

Children of WILLIAM WHITAKER and ELIZABETH CARLETON are:

     i.   LYDIA² WHITAKER, b. 1724.

    ii.   MARCUS WHITAKER, b. 1727.

   iii. SUSANNAH WHITAKER, b. 1728.

   iv. SAMUEL WHITAKER, b. 1731.

2.   v.   PETER WHITAKER, SR., b. 1732, Pennsylvania; d. 1815, Buncombe County, NC.

   vi. JR WILLIAM, WHITAKER, b. 1734, Rowan County, NC; d. 1820, Rowan County, NC; m. (1) ABIGAIL DONAHUE; b. 1740, Rowan County, NC; d. 1770, Rowan County, NC; m. (2) ABIGAIL BAKER, August 13, 1772, Whitaker's Methodist Meeting House, Mocksville, NC; b. 1750, Rowan County, NC; d. 1842, Rowan County, NC.

More About JR WILLIAM, WHITAKER:
Burial: 1820, Rowan County, NC

More About ABIGAIL DONAHUE:
Burial: 1770, Rowan County, NC

More About ABIGAIL BAKER:
Burial: 1842, Whitaker's Methodist Meeting House Cemetery, Mocksville, Rowan County, NC

More About JR WILLIAM and ABIGAIL BAKER:
Marriage: August 13, 1772, Whitaker's Methodist Meeting House, Mocksville, NC

   vii. JOSHUA WHITAKER, b. 1735.

  viii. SARAH WHITAKER, b. 1737.

   ix. JANE WHITAKER, b. 1738.

Generation No. 2

2. PETER[2] WHITAKER, SR. *(WILLIAM[1])* was born 1732 in Pennsylvania, and died 1815 in Buncombe County, NC. He married (1) ANNIE TRANTHAM 1755 in Ashe County, NC. She was born 1738 in Pennsylvania, and died 1766 in Buncombe County, NC. He married (2) LOWRAHOMA PADGETT August 08, 1767. She was born 1740. He married (3) MIRIAM F. KENT 1776, daughter of JOHN KENT and MARY.

Notes for PETER WHITAKER, SR.:
Peter Whitaker, Sr., moved from Rowan County, NC to Buncombe County, NC in 1803. He lived on Cane Creek, by his brothers Joshua, James and William.

More About PETER WHITAKER, SR.:
Burial: 1815, Buncombe County, NC

More About ANNIE TRANTHAM:
Burial: 1766, Cane Creek Cemetery, Buncombe County, NC

More About PETER WHITAKER and ANNIE TRANTHAM:
Marriage: 1755, Ashe County, NC

More About PETER WHITAKER and LOWRAHOMA PADGETT:
Marriage: August 08, 1767

More About PETER WHITAKER and MIRIAM KENT:
Marriage: 1776

Children of PETER WHITAKER and ANNIE TRANTHAM are:
3.   i.   PETER[3] WHITAKER, b. 1755, Jesey Settlement, Rowan County, NC; d. 1842, Clay County, KY.
      ii.   NOAH WHITAKER, b. 1770.
      iii. SUSANNAH WHITAKER, b. 1777.

iv.   JANE WHITAKER, b. 1781.

v.   ELIZABETH WHITAKER, b. 1785.

vi.   MIRIAM WHITAKER, b. 1786.

vii. JOHN WHITAKER, b. 1788.

Generation No. 3

3. PETER[3] WHITAKER *(PETER[2], WILLIAM[1])* was born 1755 in Jesey Settlement, Rowan County, NC, and died 1842 in Clay County, KY.

More About PETER WHITAKER:
Burial: 1842, Clay County, KY

Children of PETER WHITAKER are:

4.   i.   ISAAC[4] WHITAKER, b. 1778, Rowan County, NC; d. Clay County, KY.

     ii. EDMOND WHITAKER, b. 1779.

Generation No. 4

4. ISAAC[4] WHITAKER *(PETER[3], PETER[2], WILLIAM[1])* was born 1778 in Rowan County, NC, and died in Clay County, KY. He married SUSANNAH HARRIS 1799 in Orange County, NC. She was born 1780 in Orange County, NC, and died in Clay County, KY.

Notes for ISAAC WHITAKER:
Isaac Whitaker was instrumental in forming the first Baptist Church in Clay County, KY, in 1810. The Church was the Indian Bottom Baptist Church. Isaac Whitaker was elected first Secretary, and Electious Thompson was chosen as Pastor.

More About SUSANNAH HARRIS:
Burial: Clay County, KY

More About ISAAC WHITAKER and SUSANNAH HARRIS:
Marriage: 1799, Orange County, NC

Children of ISAAC WHITAKER and SUSANNAH HARRIS are:
- i. JOHN[5] WHITAKER, b. 1799.
- ii. ISAAC WHITAKER, b. 1801.
- iii. SAMUEL WHITAKER, b. 1802.
- iv. ELIZABETH WHITAKER, b. 1803.
- v. WILLIAM WHITAKER, b. 1803.
5. vi. PETER WHITAKER, b. July 18, 1805, Ashe County, NC; d. 1879, Clay County, KY.
- vii. SUSANNAH WHITAKER, b. 1808.
- viii. SARAH WHITAKER, b. 1809.
- ix. ESQUIRE WHITAKER, b. 1813.

Generation No. 5

5. PETER[5] WHITAKER (*ISAAC[4], PETER[3], PETER[2], WILLIAM[1]*) was born July 18, 1805 in Ashe County, NC, and died 1879 in Clay County, KY. He married DELILAH REDWINE NOE. She was born 1810 in Clay County, KY, and died 1886 in Clay County, KY.

More About PETER WHITAKER:
Burial: 1879, Clay County, KY

More About DELILAH REDWINE NOE:
Burial: 1886, Clay County, KY

Children of PETER WHITAKER and DELILAH NOE are:
6. i. EDWARD[6] WHITAKER, b. 1829, KY; d. 1892, Grayson County, KY.
- ii. ISAAC WHITAKER, b. 1832.
- iii. SARAH WHITAKER, b. 1835.

iv.   CHARLOTTE WHITAKER, b. 1837.

v.   MARY WHITAKER, b. 1840.

vi.   JANE WHITAKER, b. 1843.

vii. LAVINIA WHITAKER, b. 1845.

viii. CLARINDA WHITAKER, b. 1849.

Generation No. 6

6. EDWARD[6] WHITAKER *(PETER[5], ISAAC[4], PETER[3], PETER[2], WILLIAM[1])* was born 1829 in Pennsylvania, and died 1892 in Grayson County, KY. He married MARY J. GULLET 1858. She was born 1834 in Grayson County, KY, and died 1896 in Grayson County, KY.

More About EDWARD WHITAKER:
Burial: 1892, Grayson County, KY

More About MARY J. GULLET:
Burial: 1896, Grayson County, KY

More About EDWARD WHITAKER and MARY J. GULLET:
Marriage: 1858

Children of EDWARD WHITAKER and MARY GULLET are:

i.   JOHN[7] WHITAKER, b. 1859.

ii.   GEORGE WHITAKER, b. April 28, 1861, Harlan County, KY; d. May 28, 1946, Harlan County, KY; m. MARY JANE WILLIAMS; b. 1865, Harlan County, KY; d. 1950, Harlan County, KY.

      More About GEORGE WHITAKER:
      Burial: 1946, Harlan County, KY

More About MARY JANE WILLIAMS:
Burial: 1950, Harlan County, KY

    iii.   PEARLIE MAY WHITAKER, b. 1862; m. CHARLES HELTON; b. 1864.
7.   iv.   MINNIE BELLE WHITAKER, b. 1864, Tennessee; d. 1942, Bell County, KY. M. THOMAS T. SYKES
8.   v.   NANNIE WHITAKER, b. 1868, West Virginia. M. GEORGE KIRBY.
    vi.   ISAAC WHITAKER, b. 1866, Harlan County, KY; d. 1942, Harlan County, KY; m. MARTHA BAKER; b. 1870, Harlan County, KY; d. 1964, Harlan County, KY.

More About ISAAC WHITAKER:
Burial: 1942, Harlan County, KY

More About MARTHA BAKER:
Burial: 1964, Harlan County, KY

    vii.   MARION WHITAKER, b. 1868.
    viii.   RICHARD WHITAKER, b. 1869.
    ix.   ALABAMA WHITAKER, b. 1870.

Generation No. 7

7. MINNIE BELLE[7] WHITAKER (*EDWARD*[6], *PETER*[5], *ISAAC*[4], *PETER*[3], *PETER*[2], *WILLIAM*[1]) was born 1864 in Tennessee, and died 1942 in Bell County, KY. She married (1) MILTON P. WILLIAMS. She married (2) THOMAS TIDWELL SYKES October 04, 1907 in Wise County, VA, son of WILEY THOMAS SYKES and SUSAN TIDWELL "BITHA" BROWN. Author's Note: I believe Susan B. Brown to be the daughter of John Brown and Mahala Tidwell, but have no hard proof. Also, on the 1880 Census, she is shown as Susan T. Sykes. That could be her proper name, and "Bitha" is just a nickname.

THOMAS T. SYKES was born February 06, 1867 in Hawkins County, TN, and died 1936 in Bell County, KY.

More About MINNIE BELLE WHITAKER:
Burial: 1942, Turner Cemetery, Middlesboro, KY

Notes for THOMAS TIDWELL SYKES:
Thomas Tidwell Sykes lists his parents on his marriage license as Wiley Thomas Sykes and Susan B. Sykes. Her name is Susan Bitha Brown Sykes. Wiley T. Sykes served in the 10th. TN Volunteers, USA, in the Civil War.

More About THOMAS TIDWELL SYKES:
Burial: 1936, Turner Cemetery, Middlesboro, KY

More About THOMAS SYKES and MINNIE WHITAKER:
Marriage: October 04, 1907, Wise County, VA

Children of MINNIE WHITAKER and THOMAS SYKES are:
    i.   GRACE WILLIAMS[8] SYKES, b. 1897, Knox County, KY; d. 1990, Bell County, KY; m. ROBERT TURNER, November 06, 1920, Bell County, KY; b. 1890, Knox County, KY; d. 1982, Bell County, KY.

        More About ROBERT TURNER and GRACE SYKES:
        Marriage: November 06, 1920, Bell County, KY

    ii.   WILLIAM WILLIAMS SYKES, b. 1904, Bell County, KY; d. 1985, Ohio; m. LUCY RAINS, September 24, 1929, Bell County, KY; b. 1911, Bell County, KY; d. 1996, Ohio.

        More About WILLIAM SYKES and LUCY RAINS:
        Marriage: September 24, 1929, Bell County, KY

9. iii. NANCY WHITAKER SYKES, b. 1909, Claiborne County, TN; d. 1973, Bell County, KY.

iv. LEONA SYKES, b. 1914.

8. NANCY "NANNIE"[7] WHITAKER (*EDWARD*[6], *PETER*[5], *ISAAC*[4], *PETER*[3], *PETER*[2], *WILLIAM*[1]) was born 1868 in West Virginia. She married GEORGE KIRBY. He was born 1867 in Knox County, KY.

Children of NANNIE WHITAKER and GEORGE KIRBY are:

i. GERTRUDE[8] KIRBY, b. 1895.

ii. SHERMAN KIRBY, b. 1897.

iii. CHARLES "RED" KIRBY, b. 1899; d. 1973, Lexington, KY; m. SARAH KING; d. 1960, Harlan County, KY.

iv. JULIA KATHERINE KIRBY, b. May 22, 1904.

Generation No. 8

9. NANCY WHITAKER[8] SYKES (*MINNIE BELLE*[7] *WHITAKER*, *EDWARD*[6], *PETER*[5], *ISAAC*[4], *PETER*[3], *PETER*[2], *WILLIAM*[1]) was born 1909 in Claiborne County, TN, and died 1973 in Bell County, KY. She married WILLIAM MCKINLEY RAINS October 09, 1920 in Claiborne County, TN, son of PRESTON RAINS and CORDELIA TURNER. He was born October 12, 1900 in Bell County, KY, and died 1985 in Bell County, KY.

More About NANCY WHITAKER SYKES:
Burial: 1973, Yeary Cemetery, Middlesboro, KY

More About WILLIAM MCKINLEY RAINS:
Burial: 1985, Yeary Cemetery, Middlesboro, KY

Marriage Notes for NANCY SYKES and WILLIAM RAINS:
Married by Reverend Brad Lowery

More About WILLIAM RAINS and NANCY SYKES:
Marriage: October 09, 1920, Claiborne County, TN

Children of NANCY SYKES and WILLIAM RAINS are:

	i.	LILLIAN[9] RAINS, b. January 07, 1922, Bell County, KY; d. June 25, 1936, Bell County, KY.
10.	ii.	MABEL GRACE RAINS, b. 1922, Bell County, KY.
11.	iii.	THOMAS PRESTON RAINS, b. 1924, Bell County, KY; d. Bell County, KY.
12.	iv.	LEONA PRISCILLA RAINS, b. 1928, Bell County, KY.
	v.	MAMIE ELLEN RAINS, b. 1932, Bell County, KY; d. 1933, Bell County, KY.
13.	vi.	PAUL MCKINLEY RAINS, b. 1933, Bell County, KY; d. 1993, Covington, KY.
14.	vii.	DAVID SCHULTZ RAINS, b. August 27, 1938, Bell County, KY.
15.	viii.	ESTHER LOU RAINS, b. 1940, Bell County, KY.
16.	ix.	BILL CASPER RAINS, b. 1942, Bell County, KY.
17.	x.	JACK EDWARD RAINS, b. 1944, Bell County, KY.
18.	xi.	LINDA SUE RAINS, b. 1946, Bell County, KY.
19.	xii.	TONI LEAH RAINS, b. February 14, 1950, Bell County, KY.
20.	xiii.	JIMMIE RANDALL RAINS, b. 1952, Bell County, KY.

Generation No. 9

10. MABEL GRACE[9] RAINS (*NANCY WHITAKER*[8] *SYKES, MINNIE BELLE*[7] *WHITAKER, EDWARD*[6], *PETER*[5], *ISAAC*[4], *PETER*[3], *PETER*[2], *WILLIAM*[1]) was born 1922 in Bell County, KY. She married (1) JACOB FRANCIS MILLIGAN 1945 in Bell County, KY, son of WILLIAM MILLIGAN and DAISY COLLINS. He was born 1920 in Bell County, KY, and died 1985 in Hamilton County, Ohio. She married (2) VIRGIL DAVIS, son of WILLIAM ROSCOE DAVIS and RHODA PETREY

More About JACOB MILLIGAN and MABEL RAINS:
Marriage: 1945, Bell County, KY

Children of MABEL RAINS and JACOB MILLIGAN are:

i. JAMES JACOB[10] MILLIGAN, b. 1946, Middlesboro, Bell County, KY; m. AUDRIE MARKHAM; b. 1948, Middlesboro, Bell County, KY.

ii. BONNIE LEAH MILLIGAN, b. 1948. Married CARL GIBBS

11. THOMAS PRESTON[9] RAINS *(NANCY WHITAKER[8] SYKES, MINNIE BELLE[7] WHITAKER, EDWARD[6], PETER[5], ISAAC[4], PETER[3], PETER[2], WILLIAM[1])* was born 1924 in Bell County, KY, and died in Bell County, KY. He married EDITH MOYERS October 31, 1949 in Bell County, KY, daughter of WILLIAM MOYERS and MATILDA SOWDERS. She was born 1931 in Bell County, KY.

More About THOMAS RAINS and EDITH MOYERS:
Marriage: October 31, 1949, Bell County, KY

Children of THOMAS RAINS and EDITH MOYERS are:

i. PATRICIA[10] RAINS, b. 1950.

ii. THOMAS RAINS, b. 1952.

iii. AUDIE RAINS, b. 1953.

iv. WILLIAM RAINS, b. 1955.

v. TERRY RAINS, b. 1958.

vi. NANCY RAINS, b. 1962.

vii. LARRY RAINS, b. 1963.

viii. EDWARD RAINS, b. 1966.

ix. JAMES RAINS, b. 1967.

12. LEONA PRISCILLA[9] RAINS *(NANCY WHITAKER[8] SYKES, MINNIE BELLE[7] WHITAKER, EDWARD[6], PETER[5], ISAAC[4], PETER[3], PETER[2], WILLIAM[1])* was born 1928 in Bell County,

KY. She married RAYMOND AUGUSTUS STEINMETZ 1948 in Bell County, KY. He was born 1926 in Kentucky, and died 1998 in Covington, KY.

Notes for RAYMOND AUGUSTUS STEINMETZ:
The first mention of the name Steinmetz is Valentin Steinmetz, came from Rotterdam on the Galley St. Andrew, with John Stedman, Captain. Landed in America September 26, 1737.

More About RAYMOND STEINMETZ and LEONA RAINS:
Marriage: 1948, Bell County, KY

Children of LEONA RAINS and RAYMOND STEINMETZ are:
- i.   PAMELA SUE[10] STIENMETZ.
- ii.   PEGGY STIENMETZ, m. STAGGE.
- iii. MARK STIENMETZ.
- iv.   DOUGLAS STIENMETZ.
- v.   GREGORY STIENMETZ.
- vi.   SANDRA STIENMETZ.

13. PAUL MCKINLEY[9] RAINS (*NANCY WHITAKER[8] SYKES, MINNIE BELLE[7] WHITAKER, EDWARD[6], PETER[5], ISAAC[4], PETER[3], PETER[2], WILLIAM[1]*) was born 1933 in Bell County, KY, and died 1993 in Covington, KY. He married MILLIE MORGAN 1955 in Bell County, KY. She was born 1937 in Kentucky.

More About PAUL RAINS and MILLIE MORGAN:
Marriage: 1955, Bell County, KY

Children of PAUL RAINS and MILLIE MORGAN are:
- i.   PAUL[10] RAINS.
- ii.   DARLENE RAINS.
- iii. MALINDA RAINS.

iv.   LARRY RAINS.

v.   EDWARD RAINS

14. DAVID SCHULTZ[9] RAINS *(NANCY WHITAKER[8] SYKES, MINNIE BELLE[7] WHITAKER, EDWARD[6], PETER[5], ISAAC[4], PETER[3], PETER[2], WILLIAM[1])* was born August 27, 1938 in Bell County, KY. He married (1) EILEEN JULIANNA SIDARAS April 21, 1957 in Claiborne County, TN, daughter of STANISLAUS SIDARAS and HELEN YODIS. She was born July 30, 1938 in Kaunas, Lithuania. He married (2) SUZIE ANDERSON SHERMER September 10, 1980 in Winston-Salem, NC, daughter of EULIUS SHERMER and ALMA ANDERSON. She was born May 26, 1954 in Advance, Davie County, NC.

Notes for EILEEN JULIANNA SIDARAS:
Eileen was daughter to Stanislaus Sidaras and Helen Yodis.

More About DAVID RAINS and EILEEN SIDARAS:
Marriage: April 21, 1957, Claiborne County, TN

Notes for SUZIE ANDERSON SHERMER:
Suzie was delivered in Rowan Memorial Hospital May 26, 1953, by Dr. Henry Shaw Anderson.

More About DAVID RAINS and SUZIE SHERMER:
Marriage: September 10, 1980, Winston-Salem, NC

Children of DAVID RAINS and EILEEN SIDARAS are:

21.   i.   MICHAEL BARTHOLOMEW[10] RAINS, b. September 20, 1959, Cincinnati, Ohio.

22.   ii.   JENNIFER HELENE RAINS, b. May 26, 1962, Phoenix, Arizona.

       iii.   DANIEL PHILLIP RAINS, b. October 13, 1965, Miami, Florida.

15. ESTHER LOU[9] RAINS *(NANCY WHITAKER[8] SYKES, MINNIE BELLE[7] WHITAKER, EDWARD[6], PETER[5], ISAAC[4], PETER[3], PETER[2], WILLIAM[1])* was born 1940 in Bell County, KY. She married (1) JACK STANLEY 1957 in Bell County, KY. He was born 1934 in Bell County, KY. She married (2) JESSE MORGAN 1990, son of ERMAN MORGAN and LAURA SULFRIGE. He was born 1934 in Knox County, KY.

More About JACK STANLEY and ESTHER RAINS:
Marriage: 1957, Bell County, KY

More About JESSE MORGAN and ESTHER RAINS:
Marriage: 1990

Children of ESTHER RAINS and JACK STANLEY are:
- i. BILLY JAY[10] STANLEY.
- ii. MONA LISA STANLEY.
- iii. SONDRA STANLEY.
- iv. LARRY DEAN STANLEY.
- v. KEITH LEE STANLEY.
- vi. JOY KATHLEEN STANLEY.

16. BILL CASPER[9] RAINS *(NANCY WHITAKER[8] SYKES, MINNIE BELLE[7] WHITAKER, EDWARD[6], PETER[5], ISAAC[4], PETER[3], PETER[2], WILLIAM[1])* was born 1942 in Bell County, KY. He married ANN BROOKS in Bell County, KY. She was born 1944 in Bell County, KY.

More About BILL RAINS and ANN BROOKS:
Marriage: Bell County, KY

Children of BILL RAINS and ANN BROOKS are:
- i. MICHAEL[10] RAINS.
- ii. LISA "MISSY" RAINS.

17. JACK EDWARD[9] RAINS (*NANCY WHITAKER*[8] *SYKES, MINNIE BELLE*[7] *WHITAKER, EDWARD*[6], *PETER*[5], *ISAAC*[4], *PETER*[3], *PETER*[2], *WILLIAM*[1]) was born 1944 in Bell County, KY. He married EILEEN DANIELS. She was born 1948 in Bell County, KY.

Children of JACK RAINS and EILEEN DANIELS are:
    i.   VICKIE[10] RAINS.
    ii.   VALORIE RAINS.
    iii. RHONDA RAINS. She married BRYAN BENTLEY.
    iv. JEFFREY RAINS.

18. LINDA SUE[9] RAINS (*NANCY WHITAKER*[8] *SYKES, MINNIE BELLE*[7] *WHITAKER, EDWARD*[6], *PETER*[5], *ISAAC*[4], *PETER*[3], *PETER*[2], *WILLIAM*[1]) was born 1946 in Bell County, KY. She married BENJAMIN MCCLURE. He was born 1940 in Tennessee.

Notes for LINDA SUE RAINS:
Linda Sue Rains, Ph.D., is a professor of English. Her Husband, Ben McClure, Ph.D., is a music professor. They currently teach at Bethel University, near Memphis, TN.

Children of LINDA RAINS and BENJAMIN MCCLURE are:
    i.   DAVID JOSEPH[10] MCCLURE.
    ii.   HARRIETTE ELIZABETH MCCLURE.

19. TONI LEAH[9] RAINS (*NANCY WHITAKER*[8] *SYKES, MINNIE BELLE*[7] *WHITAKER, EDWARD*[6], *PETER*[5], *ISAAC*[4], *PETER*[3], *PETER*[2], *WILLIAM*[1]) was born February 14, 1950 in Bell County, KY. She married JAMES WEST. He was born June 06, 1947 in Bell County, KY.

Children of TONI RAINS and JAMES WEST are:
23.   i.   STACY LEE[10] WEST, b. August 08, 1969.
24.   ii.   LISA WEST, b. January 18, 1973, Chicago, Ill.

20. JIMMIE RANDALL[9] RAINS *(NANCY WHITAKER[8] SYKES, MINNIE BELLE[7] WHITAKER, EDWARD[6], PETER[5], ISAAC[4], PETER[3], PETER[2], WILLIAM[1])* was born 1952 in Bell County, KY. He married BRENDA HUMPHRIES in Bell County, KY. She was born 1956 in Bell County, KY.

More About JIMMIE RAINS and BRENDA HUMPHRIES:
Marriage: Bell County, KY

Children of JIMMIE RAINS and BRENDA HUMPHRIES are:
- i.   NANCY[10] RAINS.
- ii.   LAURA RAINS.
- iii. MISHA RAINS.
- iv.   CHRISTY RAINS.

Generation No. 10

21. MICHAEL BARTHOLOMEW[10] RAINS *(DAVID SCHULTZ[9], NANCY WHITAKER[8] SYKES, MINNIE BELLE[7] WHITAKER, EDWARD[6], PETER[5], ISAAC[4], PETER[3], PETER[2], WILLIAM[1])* was born September 20, 1959 in Cincinnati, Ohio. He married (1) CATHERINE SMART 1985. She was born August 15, 1958 in Wake County, NC. He married (2) JANEECE BAUMGARNER 1992.

Notes for MICHAEL BARTHOLOMEW RAINS:
Catherine Smart was the first wife of Michael B. Rains.

More About MICHAEL RAINS and CATHERINE SMART:
Marriage: 1985

More About MICHAEL RAINS and JANEECE BAUMGARNER:
Marriage: 1992

Children of MICHAEL RAINS and CATHERINE SMART are:

    i.   MICHAEL BARTHOLOMEW[11] RAINS, b. 1988.

Child of MICHAEL RAINS and JANEECE BAUMGARNER is:

    ii.   CHRISTOPHER THOMAS RAINS, b. 1997.

22. JENNIFER HELENE[10] RAINS (*DAVID SCHULTZ*[9], *NANCY WHITAKER*[8] *SYKES, MINNIE BELLE*[7] *WHITAKER, EDWARD*[6], *PETER*[5], *ISAAC*[4], *PETER*[3], *PETER*[2], *WILLIAM*[1]) was born May 26, 1962 in Phoenix, Arizona. She married DAVID BUTLER 1994 in Raleigh, NC. He was born 1953 in Raleigh, NC.

More About DAVID BUTLER and JENNIFER RAINS:

Marriage: 1994, Raleigh, NC

Child of JENNIFER RAINS and DAVID BUTLER is:

    i.   CHRYSTAL[11] BUTLER, b. 1989.

23. STACY LEE[10] WEST (*TONI LEAH*[9] *RAINS, NANCY WHITAKER*[8] *SYKES, MINNIE BELLE*[7] *WHITAKER, EDWARD*[6], *PETER*[5], *ISAAC*[4], *PETER*[3], *PETER*[2], *WILLIAM*[1]) was born August 08, 1969. He married BLONCA RODRIQUEZ.

Children of STACY WEST and BLONCA RODRIQUEZ are:

    i.   ANGELICA[11] WEST.

    ii.   ARMONDO WEST.

    iii.   TABITHA WEST.

    iv.   UNNAMED WEST.

24. LISA[10] WEST (*TONI LEAH*[9] *RAINS, NANCY WHITAKER*[8] *SYKES, MINNIE BELLE*[7] *WHITAKER, EDWARD*[6], *PETER*[5], *ISAAC*[4], *PETER*[3], *PETER*[2], *WILLIAM*[1]) was born January

18, 1973 in Chicago, Ill. She married DAVID KANA KAPAHUA, son of DAVID KAPAHUA and GLENDORA WOTTON. He was born March 20, 1971.

Children of LISA WEST and DAVID KAPAHUA are:

    i.   LISA FUGI[11] KAPAHUA, b. March 13, 1991.

    ii.   JUSTIN AHU KAPAHUA, b. June 05, 1992.

    iii. DAVID KANA KAPAHUA, b. January 17, 1995.

    iv. KAYLA KIANA KAPAHUA, b. February 05, 1996.

    v.   HANNA LELANI KAPAHUA, b. May 23, 2000.

Children of WILLIAM RAINS and NANCY SYKES are:

54.   i.   MABEL GRACE[9] RAINS, b. 1922, Bell County, KY.

       ii.   LILLIAN RAINS, b. January 07, 1922, Bell County, KY; d. June 25, 1936, Bell County, KY.

55.   iii. THOMAS PRESTON RAINS, b. 1924, Bell County, KY; d. Bell County, KY.

56.   iv. LEONA PRISCILLA RAINS, b. 1928, Bell County, KY.

       v.   MAMIE ELLEN RAINS, b. 1932, Bell County, KY; d. 1933, Bell County, KY.

57.   vi. PAUL MCKINLEY RAINS, b. 1933, Bell County, KY; d. December 14, 1993, Covington, KY.

58.   vii. DAVID SCHULTZ RAINS, b. August 27, 1938, Middlesboro, Bell County, KY.

59. viii. ESTHER LOU RAINS, b. 1940, Bell County, KY.

60.   ix. BILL CASPER RAINS, b. 1942, Bell County, KY.

61.   x.   JACK EDWARD RAINS, b. 1944, Bell County, KY.

62.   xi. LINDA SUE RAINS, b. 1946, Bell County, KY.

63.   xii. TONI LEAH RAINS, b. 1948, Bell County, KY.

64.   xiii. JIMMIE RANDALL RAINS, b. 1952, Bell County, KY.

47. EARNEST[8] RAINS *(PRESTON[7], WILLIAM BALLENGER[6], NEEDHAM[5], HENRY[4], JOHN[3], HENRY[2], HENRY[1])* was born 1902 in Bell County, KY, and died 1990 in Bell County,

KY. He married SUSIE UNDERWOOD May 31, 1927 in Bell County, KY. She died 1960 in Bell County, KY.

More About EARNEST RAINS and SUSIE UNDERWOOD:
Marriage: May 31, 1927, Bell County, KY

Children of EARNEST RAINS and SUSIE UNDERWOOD are:

    i.   ALAN[9] RAINS, b. 1929.

    ii.   FRED RAINS, b. 1940. (This is the son of Clarence Rains, Ernest's brother, whom Ernest Rains raised)

48. JOSHUA[8] RAINS (*PRESTON[7], WILLIAM BALLENGER[6], NEEDHAM[5], HENRY[4], JOHN[3], HENRY[2], HENRY[1]*) was born September 14, 1907 in Bell County, KY, and died January 12, 1997 in Bell County, KY. He married (1) GLADYS WARWICK August 09, 1934 in Bell County, KY. She was born 1912 in Bell County, KY, and died 1946 in Bell County, KY. He married (2) RACHEL ATKINS 1948.

More About JOSHUA RAINS and GLADYS WARWICK:
Marriage: August 09, 1934, Bell County, KY

More About JOSHUA RAINS and RACHEL ATKINS:
Marriage: 1948

Children of JOSHUA RAINS and GLADYS WARWICK and RACHEL ATKINS are:

    i.   ROGER[9] RAINS.

    ii.   HAROLD RAINS.

65.   iii.   DONNA RAINS.

    iv.   LOUISE RAINS, b. 1935.

    v.   BOBBIE RAINS, b. 1936.

    vi.   JUANITA RAINS, b. 1937; m. DAVID FANSLAU.

    vii.   JOSHUA RAINS,JR, b. 1941.

49. CLARENCE[8] RAINS *(PRESTON[7], WILLIAM BALLENGER[6], NEEDHAM[5], HENRY[4], JOHN[3], HENRY[2], HENRY[1])* was born 1909 in Bell County, KY, and died Aft. 1999 in Bell County, KY. He married (1) MARTHA HURST September 25, 1931 in Bell County, KY. She was born 1912 in Bell County, KY, and died in ?. He married (2) MAMIE HATFIELD June 22, 1940 in William McKinley Rains Home, Middlesboro, KY. She was born 1922 in Bell County, KY. He married (3) DIXIE LEE WHITE April 28, 1947 in The home of Rev. William McKinley Rains, Middlesboro, KY. She was born 1923 in Bell County, KY.

Notes for CLARENCE RAINS:
The wedding was performed by Clarence's brother, Rev. William McKinley Rains. Witnesses were Nelly Turner and W. P. Rains.

Marriage Notes for CLARENCE RAINS and MARTHA HURST:
Rev. William McKinley Rains, Clarence's brother, performed the ceremony.

More About CLARENCE RAINS and MARTHA HURST:
Marriage: September 25, 1931, Bell County, KY

More About CLARENCE RAINS and MAMIE HATFIELD:
Marriage: June 22, 1940, William Mckinley Rains Home, Middlesboro, KY

Marriage Notes for CLARENCE RAINS and DIXIE WHITE:
Clarence Rains' brother, the Rev. William McKinley Rains, performed the ceremony. Witnesses were Charles Spitzer and Joshua Rains.

More About CLARENCE RAINS and DIXIE WHITE:
Marriage: April 28, 1947, The home of Rev. William McKinley Rains, Middlesboro, KY

Child of CLARENCE RAINS and DIXIE WHITE is:
    i.   BRENDA[9] RAINS, b. 1954.

50. HELEN[8] RAINS *(PRESTON[7], WILLIAM BALLENGER[6], NEEDHAM[5], HENRY[4], JOHN[3], HENRY[2], HENRY[1])* was born 1913 in Bell County, KY, and died 1968 in Monroe, MI. She married (1) LOUIS NAVARRE. She married (2) ROBERT J. PARTIN March 06, 1933 in Bell County, KY. He was born 1910 in Bell County, KY.

More About ROBERT PARTIN and HELEN RAINS:
Marriage: March 06, 1933, Bell County, KY

Children of HELEN RAINS and ROBERT PARTIN are:
    i.   OLIVER[9] PARTIN.
    ii.   STELLA PARTIN.

51. AMANDA[8] RAINS *(PRESTON[7], WILLIAM BALLENGER[6], NEEDHAM[5], HENRY[4], JOHN[3], HENRY[2], HENRY[1])* was born June 15, 1915 in Bell County, KY. She married (1) JOHN FLANERY April 15, 1933 in Bell County, KY. He was born 1918 in Bell County, KY. She married (2) CLAUDE MASSENGILL 1935. He was born March 20, 1905 in Middlesboro, Bell County, KY, and died May 28, 1983 in Monroe, MI.

Notes for AMANDA RAINS:
Amanda is daughter of Nancy Simpson and Preston Rains

More About JOHN FLANERY and AMANDA RAINS:
Marriage: April 15, 1933, Bell County, KY

More About CLAUDE MASSENGILL and AMANDA RAINS:
Marriage: 1935

Children of AMANDA RAINS and CLAUDE MASSENGILL are:
    i.   THELMA[9] MASSENGILL, b. September 25, 1936; m. GEORGE MENEFEE.
66.   ii.   EUGENE EDWARD MASSENGILL, b. February 13, 1937.
67.   iii. WILLIAM GLEN MASSENGILL, b. November 19, 1939.

68. iv. SHIRLEY ANN MASSENGILL, b. June 01, 1941.

69. v.   JUANITA MASSENGILL, b. March 22, 1943.

70. vi. CLAUDE MASSENGILL, JR., b. February 19, 1945.

     vii. JAMES DAVID MASSENGILL, b. February 28, 1948.

71. viii. JERRY MICHAEL MASSENGILL, b. August 08, 1953.

52. BESSY ELIZABETH[8] RAINS *(PRESTON[7], WILLIAM BALLENGER[6], NEEDHAM[5], HENRY[4], JOHN[3], HENRY[2], HENRY[1])* was born 1920. She married WILLIE ROSS ROBSON.

Notes for BESSY ELIZABETH RAINS:

Betsy Rains is daughter of Preston Rains and Nancy Simpson.

Children of BESSY RAINS and WILLIE ROBSON are:

     i. RUBY[9] ROBSON, m. CHARLES SINDONE.

     ii. BILLIE ROBSON, m. JOHN HOLLAND.

Generation No. 8

53. AUDRIE MAE[9] RAINS *(WILLIAM RICE[8], MILTON LANE RICE[7], WILLIAM BALLENGER[6], NEEDHAM[5], HENRY[4], JOHN[3], HENRY[2], HENRY[1])* was born in Bell County, KY. She married GEORGE W. ESTEPP. He was born in Bell County, KY.

Child of AUDRIE RAINS and GEORGE ESTEPP is:

     i. SHAWN[10] ESTEPP.

54. MABEL GRACE[9] RAINS *(WILLIAM MCKINLEY[8], PRESTON[7], WILLIAM BALLENGER[6], NEEDHAM[5], HENRY[4], JOHN[3], HENRY[2], HENRY[1])* was born 1922 in Bell County, KY. She married JACOB FRANCIS MILLIGAN 1945 in Bell County, KY. He was born 1920 in Bell

County, KY, and died 1985 in Hamilton County, Ohio. Mabel Married VERGIL DAVIS, September, 1980.

More About JACOB MILLIGAN and MABEL RAINS:
Marriage: 1945, Bell County, KY

Children of MABEL RAINS and JACOB MILLIGAN are:
    i.   JACOB FRANCIS[10] MILLIGAN, b. 1946.
    ii.   BONNIE LEAH MILLIGAN, b. 1948.

55. THOMAS PRESTON[9] RAINS (*WILLIAM MCKINLEY*[8], *PRESTON*[7], *WILLIAM BALLENGER*[6], *NEEDHAM*[5], *HENRY*[4], *JOHN*[3], *HENRY*[2], *HENRY*[1]) was born 1924 in Bell County, KY, and died in Bell County, KY. He married EDITH MOYERS October 31, 1949 in Bell County, KY, daughter of WILLIAM "BIRD" MOYERS and MINNIE SOWDERS. She was born 1931 in Bell County, KY.

More About THOMAS RAINS and EDITH MOYERS:
Marriage: October 31, 1949, Bell County, KY

Children of THOMAS RAINS and EDITH MOYERS are:
    i.   PATRICIA[10] RAINS, b. 1950.
    ii.   THOMAS RAINS, b. 1952.
    iii. AUDIE RAINS, b. 1953.
    iv.   WILLIAM RAINS, b. 1955.
    v.   TERRY RAINS, b. 1958.
    vi.   NANCY RAINS, b. 1962.
    vii. LARRY RAINS, b. 1963.
    viii. EDWARD RAINS, b. 1966.
    ix.   JAMES RAINS, b. 1967.

56. LEONA PRISCILLA[9] RAINS *(WILLIAM MCKINLEY[8], PRESTON[7], WILLIAM BALLENGER[6], NEEDHAM[5], HENRY[4], JOHN[3], HENRY[2], HENRY[1])* was born 1928 in Bell County, KY. She married RAYMOND AUGUSTUS STIENMETZ 1948 in Bell County, KY. He was born 1926 in Kentucky, and died 1998 in Covington, KY.

More About RAYMOND STIENMETZ and LEONA RAINS:
Marriage: 1948, Bell County, KY

Children of LEONA RAINS and RAYMOND STIENMETZ are:
  i.   PAMELA SUE[10] STIENMETZ.
  ii.   PEGGY STIENMETZ.
  iii. MARK STIENMETZ.
  iv.   DOUGLAS STIENMETZ.
  v.   GREGORY STIENMETZ.
  vi.   SANDRA STIENMETZ.

57. PAUL MCKINLEY[9] RAINS *(WILLIAM MCKINLEY[8], PRESTON[7], WILLIAM BALLENGER[6], NEEDHAM[5], HENRY[4], JOHN[3], HENRY[2], HENRY[1])* was born 1933 in Bell County, KY, and died December 14, 1993 in Covington, KY. He married MILLIE MORGAN 1955 in Bell County, KY. She was born 1937 in Kentucky.

More About PAUL MCKINLEY RAINS:
Burial: December 16, 1993, Covington, KY

More About PAUL RAINS and MILLIE MORGAN:
Marriage: 1955, Bell County, KY

Children of PAUL RAINS and MILLIE MORGAN are:
  i.   PAUL[10] RAINS.
  ii.   DARLENE RAINS.
  iii. MALINDA RAINS.

iv.   EDWARD RAINS.

v.   LARRY RAINS.

58. DAVID SCHULTZ[9] RAINS (*WILLIAM MCKINLEY*[8], *PRESTON*[7], *WILLIAM BALLENGER*[6], *NEEDHAM*[5], *HENRY*[4], *JOHN*[3], *HENRY*[2], *HENRY*[1]) was born August 27, 1938 in Middlesboro, Bell County, KY. He married (1) EILEEN JULIANNA SIDARAS April 21, 1957 in Claiborne County, TN, daughter of STANISLAUS SIDARAS and HELEN YODIS. She was born July 30, 1938 in Elizabeth, NJ. He married (2) SUZIE ANDERSON SHERMER September 10, 1980 in Winston-Salem, NC, daughter of EULIUS SHERMER and ALMA ANDERSON. She was born May 26, 1954 in Advance, Davie County, NC.

More About DAVID RAINS and EILEEN SIDARAS:
Marriage: April 21, 1957, Claiborne County, TN

Notes for SUZIE ANDERSON SHERMER:
Suzie was delivered in Rowan Memorial Hospital May 26, 1953, by Dr. Henry Shaw Anderson. Suzie was stepmother to Michael Bartholomew Rains, Jennifer Helene Rains, and Daniel Phillip Rains, children to her husband, David S. Rains, by Eileen Julianne Sidaras.

More About DAVID RAINS and SUZIE SHERMER:
Marriage: September 10, 1980, Winston-Salem, NC

Children of DAVID RAINS and EILEEN SIDARAS are:

72.   i.   MICHAEL BARTHOLOMEW[10] RAINS, b. September 20, 1959, Cincinnati, Ohio.

73.   ii.   JENNIFER HELENE RAINS, b. May 26, 1962, Phoenix, Arizona.

       iii.   DANIEL PHILLIP RAINS, b. October 13, 1965, Miami, Florida.

59. ESTHER LOU[9] RAINS (*WILLIAM MCKINLEY*[8], *PRESTON*[7], *WILLIAM BALLENGER*[6], *NEEDHAM*[5], *HENRY*[4], *JOHN*[3], *HENRY*[2], *HENRY*[1]) was born 1940 in Bell County, KY. She married (1) JACK STANLEY 1957 in Bell County, KY. He was born 1934 in Bell County, KY. She married (2) JESSE MORGAN 1990, son of ERMAN MORGAN and LAURA SUL-FRIGE. He was born 1934 in Knox County, KY.

More About JACK STANLEY and ESTHER RAINS:
Marriage: 1957, Bell County, KY

More About JESSE MORGAN and ESTHER RAINS:
Marriage: 1990

Children of ESTHER RAINS and JACK STANLEY are:
  i.   BILLY JAY[10] STANLEY.
  ii.   MONA LISA STANLEY.
  iii. SONDRA STANLEY.
  iv.   LARRY DEAN STANLEY.
  v.   KEITH LEE STANLEY.
  vi.   JOY KATHLEEN STANLEY.

60. BILL CASPER[9] RAINS (*WILLIAM MCKINLEY*[8], *PRESTON*[7], *WILLIAM BALLENGER*[6], *NEEDHAM*[5], *HENRY*[4], *JOHN*[3], *HENRY*[2], *HENRY*[1]) was born 1942 in Bell County, KY. He married ANN BROOKS in Bell County, KY. She was born 1944 in Bell County, KY.

More About BILL RAINS and ANN BROOKS:
Marriage: Bell County, KY

Children of BILL RAINS and ANN BROOKS are:
  i.   MICHAEL[10] RAINS.
  ii.   MISSY RAINS.

61. JACK EDWARD[9] RAINS *(WILLIAM MCKINLEY[8], PRESTON[7], WILLIAM BALLENGER[6], NEEDHAM[5], HENRY[4], JOHN[3], HENRY[2], HENRY[1])* was born 1944 in Bell County, KY. He married EILEEN DANIELS. She was born 1948 in Bell County, KY.

Children of JACK RAINS and EILEEN DANIELS are:
   i.   VICKIE[10] RAINS.
   ii.   VALORIE RAINS.
   iii. RHONDA RAINS.
   iv.   JEFFREY RAINS.

62. LINDA SUE[9] RAINS *(WILLIAM MCKINLEY[8], PRESTON[7], WILLIAM BALLENGER[6], NEEDHAM[5], HENRY[4], JOHN[3], HENRY[2], HENRY[1])* was born 1946 in Bell County, KY. She married BENJAMIN MCCLURE. He was born 1940 in Tennessee.

Notes for LINDA SUE RAINS:
Linda Sue Rains, Ph.D, is a professor of English. Her Husband, Ben McClure, Ph.D., is a music professor. They currently teach at Bethel University, near Memphis, TN.

Children of LINDA RAINS and BENJAMIN MCCLURE are:
   i.   DAVID JOSEPH[10] MCCLURE.
   ii.   HARRIETTE ELIZABETH MCCLURE.

63. TONI LEAH[9] RAINS *(WILLIAM MCKINLEY[8], PRESTON[7], WILLIAM BALLENGER[6], NEEDHAM[5], HENRY[4], JOHN[3], HENRY[2], HENRY[1])* was born 1948 in Bell County, KY. She married JAMES WEST. He was born 1946 in Bell County, KY.

Children of TONI RAINS and JAMES WEST are:
   i.   STACY LEE[10] WEST.
   ii.   LISA WEST.

64. JIMMIE RANDALL[9] RAINS *(WILLIAM MCKINLEY[8], PRESTON[7], WILLIAM BALLENGER[6], NEEDHAM[5], HENRY[4], JOHN[3], HENRY[2], HENRY[1])* was born 1952 in Bell County, KY. He married BRENDA HUMPHRIES in Bell County, KY. She was born 1956 in Bell County, KY.

More About JIMMIE RAINS and BRENDA HUMPHRIES:
Marriage: Bell County, KY

Children of JIMMIE RAINS and BRENDA HUMPHRIES are:
- i. NANCY[10] RAINS.
- ii. LAURA RAINS.
- iii. MISHA RAINS.
- iv. CHRISTY RAINS.

65. DONNA[9] RAINS *(JOSHUA[8], PRESTON[7], WILLIAM BALLENGER[6], NEEDHAM[5], HENRY[4], JOHN[3], HENRY[2], HENRY[1])* She married ROBERT C. ELLISON.

Children of DONNA RAINS and ROBERT ELLISON are:
- i. MELISSA MARIE[10] ELLISON.
- ii. RACHEL ANN ELLISON.

   Notes for RACHEL ANN ELLISON:
   This child died at birth.

- iii. ROBERT MATTHEW ELLISON.
- iv. STEVEN ALLEN ELLISON.

66. EUGENE EDWARD[9] MASSENGILL *(AMANDA[8] RAINS, PRESTON[7], WILLIAM BALLENGER[6], NEEDHAM[5], HENRY[4], JOHN[3], HENRY[2], HENRY[1])* was born February 13, 1937. He married DIANE MCBRIDE. She was born 1940.

Children of EUGENE MASSENGILL and DIANE MCBRIDE are:

    i.   CHERYL[10] MASSENGILL.

    ii.   EUGENE MASSENGILL.

    iii. JAMES MASSENGILL.

67. WILLIAM GLEN[9] MASSENGILL *(AMANDA[8] RAINS, PRESTON[7], WILLIAM BALLENGER[6], NEEDHAM[5], HENRY[4], JOHN[3], HENRY[2], HENRY[1])* was born November 19, 1939. He married LINDA.

Child of WILLIAM MASSENGILL and LINDA is:

    i.   WILLIAM JACK[10] MASSENGILL.

68. SHIRLEY ANN[9] MASSENGILL *(AMANDA[8] RAINS, PRESTON[7], WILLIAM BALLENGER[6], NEEDHAM[5], HENRY[4], JOHN[3], HENRY[2], HENRY[1])* was born June 01, 1941. She married JAMES BORNEA.

Children of SHIRLEY MASSENGILL and JAMES BORNEA are:

    i.   BRENT[10] BORNEA.

    ii.   JILL BORNEA.

69. JUANITA[9] MASSENGILL *(AMANDA[8] RAINS, PRESTON[7], WILLIAM BALLENGER[6], NEEDHAM[5], HENRY[4], JOHN[3], HENRY[2], HENRY[1])* was born March 22, 1943. She married RALPH D. SMITH.

Child of JUANITA MASSENGILL and RALPH SMITH is:

    i.   RENEE[10] SMITH.

70. CLAUDE[9] MASSENGILL, JR. *(AMANDA[8] RAINS, PRESTON[7], WILLIAM BALLENGER[6], NEEDHAM[5], HENRY[4], JOHN[3], HENRY[2], HENRY[1])* was born February 19, 1945. He married (1) REBECCA MIRACLE. He married (2) MARY KAY DIROFF JENNEWINE December 26, 1994. She was born October 10, 1949.

More About CLAUDE MASSENGILL and MARY JENNEWINE:
Marriage: December 26, 1994

Children of CLAUDE MASSENGILL and REBECCA MIRACLE are:
    i.   JOHN CLAUDE[10] MASSENGILL, b. March 15, 1974.
    ii.   JULIE ROSE MASSENGILL, b. April 15, 1976.

71. JERRY MICHAEL[9] MASSENGILL *(AMANDA[8] RAINS, PRESTON[7], WILLIAM BALLENGER[6], NEEDHAM[5], HENRY[4], JOHN[3], HENRY[2], HENRY[1])* was born August 08, 1953. He married DEBRA MCBRIDE.

Children of JERRY MASSENGILL and DEBRA MCBRIDE are:
    i.   ANGELA[10] MASSENGILL.
    ii.   CLAUDE MICHAEL MASSENGILL.

Generation No. 9

72. MICHAEL BARTHOLOMEW[10] RAINS *(DAVID SCHULTZ[9], WILLIAM MCKINLEY[8], PRESTON[7], WILLIAM BALLENGER[6], NEEDHAM[5], HENRY[4], JOHN[3], HENRY[2], HENRY[1])* was born September 20, 1959 in Cincinnati, Ohio. He married (1) CATHERINE SMART 1985. She was born August 15, 1958 in Wake County, NC. He married (2) JANEECE BAUMGARNER 1992.

Notes for MICHAEL BARTHOLOMEW RAINS:
Catherine Smart was the first wife of Michael B. Rains.

More About MICHAEL RAINS and CATHERINE SMART:
Marriage: 1985

More About MICHAEL RAINS and JANEECE BAUMGARNER:
Marriage: 1992

Children of MICHAEL RAINS and CATHERINE SMART are:
   i.   MICHAEL BARTHOLOMEW[11] RAINS, b. September 19, 1988.
   ii.   CHRISTOPHER THOMAS RAINS, b. June 03, 1997.

73. JENNIFER HELENE[10] RAINS *(DAVID SCHULTZ[9], WILLIAM MCKINLEY[8], PRESTON[7], WILLIAM BALLENGER[6], NEEDHAM[5], HENRY[4], JOHN[3], HENRY[2], HENRY[1])* was born May 26, 1962 in Phoenix, Arizona. She married (1) ROBERT PARSONS. He was born 1956 in Johnston County, NC, and died 1997 in NC. She married (2) SCOTT KENNEDY. He was born 1958 in Raleigh, Wake County, NC. She married (3) DAVID BUTLER 1994 in Raleigh, NC. He was born 1953 in Raleigh, NC.

Notes for JENNIFER HELENE RAINS:
Jennifer Helene Rains was the stepmother of Chrystal Butler. Jennifer had no children of her own.

More About DAVID BUTLER and JENNIFER RAINS:
Marriage: 1994, Raleigh, NC

Child of JENNIFER RAINS and DAVID BUTLER is:
   i.   CHRYSTAL[11] BUTLER, b. 1989.

AUTHORS NOTE: I know there are duplications of individuals from including the descendants of the Whitaker and Turner families, and I ask you to overlook them in the interest of including as many converging family lines as possible.

Here is what I have gathered on the Peter SCHIRMER (Shermer) family of my wife, Suzie Anderson Shermer Rains:

CHAPTER 14

Rains and Shermer Families

Descendants of Martin Schirmer

Who probably comes from Rupertus Schirmer, **ca. 1100 A.D.**
And Schirmer Von Stolzenfels, **of Kassel, Germany**

Generation No. 1
Note: "Schirmer" means "Protector" in German.

1. MARTIN[1] SCHIRMER was born Abt. 1600 in Undenheim, Rheinhessen, Germany, and died April 15, 1675 in Undenheim, Rheinhessen, Germany. He married CATHARINA Abt. 1624 in Undensheim, Rheinhessen, Germany. She was born Abt. 1610 in Undenheim, Rheinhessen, Germany.

More About MARTIN SCHIRMER:
Burial: Undenheim, Rheinhessen, Germany

Children of MARTIN SCHIRMER and CATHARINA are:
    i.   MARGARETHA[2] SCHIRMER, b. 1634.
    ii.   CATHERINA SCHIRMER, b. 1643.
2.   iii. HANS MARTIN SCHIRMER, b. 1645, Undenheim, Rheinhessen, Germany; d. Aft. 1699, Undenheim, Rheinhessen, Germany.

iv.   ANDREAS SCHIRMER, b. 1653.

v.   GERTRAUT SCHIRMER, b. 1655.

Generation No. 2

2. HANS MARTIN[2] SCHIRMER *(MARTIN[1])* was born 1645 in Undenheim, Rheinhessen, Germany, and died Aft. 1699 in Undenheim, Rheinhessen, Germany. He married ANNA ELIZABETH ARNSHEIMER May 13, 1673 in Undensheim, Rheinhessen, Germany. She was born January 1651/52 in Undenheim, Rheinhessen, Germany, and died Aft. 1699 in Undenheim, Rheinhessen, Germany.

More About HANS MARTIN SCHIRMER:
Burial: Undenheim, Rheinhessen, Germany

More About ANNA ELIZABETH ARNSHEIMER:
Burial: Undenheim, Rheinhessen, Germany

Children of HANS SCHIRMER and ANNA ARNSHEIMER are:

i.   JOHANNES MARTIN[3] SCHIRMER, b. 1677.

ii.   VOLPERT SCHIRMER, b. 1682.

      Notes for VOLPERT SCHIRMER:
      Undenheim Reformed Church Book Notes, 1441-1984. Note NS50733

3.   iii. JOHANN JACOB SCHIRMER, b. June 28, 1683, Undenheim, Rheinhessen, Germany.

iv.   ANNA CATHERINA SCHIRMER, b. 1686.

v.   ANNA MARGARETHA SCHIRMER, b. 1689.

vi.   ANNA ELIZABETH SCHIRMER, b. 1690.

Generation No. 3

3. JOHANN JACOB[3] SCHIRMER *(HANS MARTIN[2], MARTIN[1])* was born June 28, 1683 in Undenheim, Rheinhessen, Germany. He married ANNA CATHARINA.

Children of JOHANN SCHIRMER and ANNA CATHARINA are:

    i.   MARY MAGDALENA[4] SCHIRMER, m. DEWALD DIEL, 1754, Philadelphia, Penna..

    ii.   GEORGE JACOB SCHIRMER, b. March 03, 1729/30, Winden, Germany; m. GERTRUDE DORFLINGER.

    Notes for GEORGE JACOB SCHIRMER:
    Arrived on the ship Janet on October 7, 1751.

4.   iii.   I PETER SCHIRMER, b. 1723, Winden, near Zweibrucken; d. 1784, Surry County N. C.info from Census 1790, will dated 1791, 1.

Generation No. 4

4. I PETER[4] SCHIRMER *(JOHANN JACOB[3], HANS MARTIN[2], MARTIN[1])* was born 1723 in Winden, near Zweibrucken, and died 1784 in Surry County N. C.info from Census 1790, will dated 1791, 1. He married MOLLY GROCE. She was born 1730.

Notes for I PETER SCHIRMER:
Peter Schirmer was born in Winden, near Zweibrucken, in Germany. He arrived in Philadelphia in August, 28, 1750, on the ship Phoenix, with Captain John Mason, with his wife Magdalena, daughter Maria Barbara and a sister named Magdalena.

More About I PETER SCHIRMER:
Burial: Surry County, NC

Children of PETER SCHIRMER and MOLLY GROCE are:

    i.   MOLLY[5] SCHIRMER.

    ii.   MARGARET SCHIRMER.

5.   iii. MARY MAGDALENE SCHIRMER, b. 1750.

    iv. CHRISTINE SCHIRMER.

    v.   MARIA BARBARA SCHIRMER, b. May 07, 1750, Winden, Germany.

    vi. CATHAREINA SCHIRMER, b. 1754, Philadelphia, Penna.; d. July 17, 1844, Surry Co. NC.

6.   vii. II PETER SCHIRMER II, b. Abt. 1760, Surry county, N.C..

Generation No. 5

5. MARY MAGDALENE[5] SCHIRMER *(PETER[4], JOHANN JACOB[3], HANS MARTIN[2], MARTIN[1])* was born 1750. She married SIMON GROSS, JR. February 13, 1770 in Rowan County, NC, son of SIMON GROSS and VERONICA MAYER. He was born 1746.

Child of MARY SCHIRMER and SIMON GROSS is:

    i.   PETER[6] GROSS.

6. II PETER[5] SCHIRMER II *(PETER[4], JOHANN JACOB[3], HANS MARTIN[2], MARTIN[1])* was born Abt. 1760 in Surry county, N.C.. He married MARY SHORES June 25, 1801 in Surry County, N. C., daughter of JACOB SHORS and MARGARET SHORS. She was born Abt. 1766 in Surry County N. C., and died 1855.

Children of PETER SCHIRMER and MARY SHORES are:

7.   i.   JOHN B.[6] SHERMER, b. November 28, 1802, Surry County N.C.; d. 1860, Buried in Surry County.

8.   ii.   III PETER SHERMER III, b. June 09, 1804, Surry County, N. C.; d. March 1881, Surry County , N.C..

Generation No. 6

7. JOHN B.[6] SHERMER *(PETER[5] SCHIRMER II, PETER[4], JOHANN JACOB[3], HANS MARTIN[2], MARTIN[1])* was born November 28, 1802 in Surry County N.C., and died 1860 in Buried in Surry County. He married CLOE GOUGH March 03, 1831, daughter of - JAMES GOUGH and CATHERINE HUTSON. She was born March 31, 1812 in Surry County, N. C., and died 1866 in Surry County N. C..

Children of JOHN SHERMER and CLOE GOUGH are:

	i.	NANCY[7] SHERMER, b. December 1831.
	ii.	MARY SHERMER, b. May 1833.
	iii.	JAS SHERMER, b. June 1835.
	iv.	FREDRICK SHERMER, b. May 1837.
	v.	NANCY SHERMER, b. November 1839.
9.	vi.	JOHN HENRY SHERMER, b. March 1842, Surry Co. N. C.; d. July 20, 1916, Allgood Family Cemetary, Yadkin County, N. C..
	vii.	ISSAC SHERMER, b. August 1844.
	viii.	PETER SHERMER, b. April 1847.
	ix.	CHLOE SHERMER, b. December 1849.
	x.	THUSY CATHRINE SHERMER, b. June 1851.
	xi.	SARY ANN SHERMER, b. February 1854.

8. III PETER[6] SHERMER III *(PETER[5] SCHIRMER II, PETER[4], JOHANN JACOB[3], HANS MARTIN[2], MARTIN[1])* was born June 09, 1804 in Surry County, N. C., and died March 1881 in Surry County , N.C.. He married MARY ELIZABETH CHINN Abt. 1823 in Surry County, N. C.. She was born May 06, 1800 in Surry County, N. C., and died July 29, 1881 in Surry County, N. C..

Notes for III PETER SHERMER III:

Buried in Shermer Cemetery, with his wife, according to the Shermer Family Bible of Sidney Shermer

More About III PETER SHERMER III:
Burial: March 1881, Shermer Cemetery, Yadkin County, NC

More About MARY ELIZABETH CHINN:
Burial: July 31, 1881, Shermer Cemetery, Yadkin County, NC

Children of PETER SHERMER and MARY CHINN are:

    i.   DAVID[7] SHERMER, b. June 15, 1825, Surry Co. N. C.; d. January 29, 1833, Surry Co. N. C..

        More About DAVID SHERMER:
        Burial: January 29, 1833, Yadkin County, NC

    ii.   WILLIAM SHERMER, b. April 20, 1830, Surry Co. N. C.; d. February 23, 1912; m. ELIZABETH PRIDDLE.
    iii.   PAULINA SHERMER, b. May 29, 1833, Surry Co. N. C.; m. IRA LYNCH.
    iv.   JOHN SHERMER, b. September 16, 1835, Surry Co. N. C.; d. March 08, 1845.
    v.   JESSE C. SHERMER, b. January 08, 1837, Surry Co, N. C.; d. July 17, 1837, Surry Co, N. C..
    vi.   LV PETER A. SHERMER, b. August 06, 1838, Surry Co. N. C.; d. May 25, 1903; m. CORDELIA SPEASE.
    vii.   JESSE SHERMER, b. January 29, 1840, Surry Co., N. C.; d. May 02, 1863.
    viii.   ELIZABETH A. SHERMER, b. June 23, 1841, Surry Co. N. C.; d. June 11, 1915; m. T. L. MACY, June 13, 1865.
    ix.   PERRY SHERMER, b. March 16, 1845, Surry Co. N. C.; d. March 17, 1929; m. LOUISE HOOTS.

Generation No. 7

9. JOHN HENRY[7] SHERMER *(JOHN B.[6], PETER[5] SCHIRMER II, PETER[4], JOHANN JACOB[3], HANS MARTIN[2], MARTIN[1])* was born March 1842 in Surry Co. N. C., and died July 20,

1916 in Allgood Family Cemetary, Yadkin County, N. C.. He married BARBARA ELIZA-BETH HUTCHENS September 16, 1865, daughter of ALEXANDER HUTCHENS and CATHERINE WISHON. She was born November 17, 1842 in Surry County. N. C., and died 1916.

Notes for JOHN HENRY SHERMER:
John Henry Shermer and his wife Elizabeth separated. John Henry Shermer left for another woman, according to family history.

Children of JOHN SHERMER and BARBARA HUTCHENS are:
    i.   LUCY[8] SHERMER, d. 1942.
    ii.   ANDREW SHERMER, b. May 21, 1866.
    iii.   NANCY CATHERINE SHERMER, b. May 21, 1866.
    iv.   NOAH A. SHERMER, b. November 15, 1868.
10.   v.   TANDY MERONEY SHERMER, b. September 29, 1869; d. July 18, 1960, Advance, N. C..
    vi.   MARY E. SHERMER, b. May 26, 1872.
    vii.   JOHN BOYD SHERMER, b. April 04, 1874.
    viii.   WILLIAM GASTON SHERMER, b. April 15, 1878; d. April 20, 1964.

Generation No. 8

10. TANDY MERONEY[8] SHERMER (*JOHN HENRY[7], JOHN B.[6], PETER[5] SCHIRMER II, PETER[4], JOHANN JACOB[3], HANS MARTIN[2], MARTIN[1]*) was born September 29, 1869, and died July 18, 1960 in Advance, N. C.. He married MINNIE LEE CATON September 28, 1899, daughter of ALFRED CATON and MARY BAILEY. She was born March 03, 1871, and died March 1961 in Advance N. C..

Children of TANDY SHERMER and MINNIE CATON are:
    i.   WILLIE JO[9] SHERMER, b. June 10, 1900; d. January 14, 1992; m. H. A. REYNOLDS.

11. ii.   ANDREW ALEXANDER SHERMER, b. February 15, 1903, Advance, N. C.; d. July 04, 1971, Richmond, Va..

12. iii. EDNA VIOLA SHERMER, b. October 28, 1905, Advance, N. C.; d. May 07, 1988, Long Island, N. Y..

13. iv.   ALPHA TELMONT SHERMER, b. July 01, 1908, Advance, N.C..

14. v.   EULIUS MERONEY SHERMER, b. March 23, 1911, Advance, N. C.; d. September 16, 1977, Advance, N. C..

15. vi.   ATLEE CATON SHERMER, b. January 01, 1914, advance N. C..

16. vii. LUCY SUSANNAH SYDRENE SHERMER, b. November 04, 1916, Advance, N.C.; d. February 13, 1975.

17. viii. JEROME QUINTON SHERMER, b. July 31, 1919, Advance, N. C.; d. April 24, 1985.

18. ix.   JULIA HENRIETTA SHERMER, b. June 10, 1922, Advance, N. C..

Generation No. 9

11. ANDREW ALEXANDER[9] SHERMER *(TANDY MERONEY[8], JOHN HENRY[7], JOHN B.[6], PETER[5] SCHIRMER II, PETER[4], JOHANN JACOB[3], HANS MARTIN[2], MARTIN[1])* was born February 15, 1903 in Advance, N. C., and died July 04, 1971 in Richmond, Va.. He married MARY ELIZABETH REYNOLDS.

Children of ANDREW SHERMER and MARY REYNOLDS are:

19. i.   MARY REYNOLDS[10] SHERMER, b. June 10, 1940, Richmond, Virginia the old Johnston Willis Hospital.

20. ii.   CATON ALEXANDER SHERMER, b. September 20, 1941, Richmond, Va. old Johnston Willis Hospital.

12. EDNA VIOLA[9] SHERMER *(TANDY MERONEY[8], JOHN HENRY[7], JOHN B.[6], PETER[5] SCHIRMER II, PETER[4], JOHANN JACOB[3], HANS MARTIN[2], MARTIN[1])* was born October

28, 1905 in Advance, N. C., and died May 07, 1988 in Long Island, N. Y.. She married ALEXANDER GROSSMAN.

Child of EDNA SHERMER and ALEXANDER GROSSMAN is:

    i.   LILLIAN[10] GROSSMAN, m. NICK ALLARD.

13. ALPHA TELMONT[9] SHERMER *(TANDY MERONEY[8], JOHN HENRY[7], JOHN B.[6], PETER[5] SCHIRMER II, PETER[4], JOHANN JACOB[3], HANS MARTIN[2], MARTIN[1])* was born July 01, 1908 in Advance, N.C.. She married JOHN VOGLER.

Children of ALPHA SHERMER and JOHN VOGLER are:

    i.   GENE[10] VOGLER.

    ii.   PEGGY VOGLER.

14. EULIUS MERONEY[9] SHERMER *(TANDY MERONEY[8], JOHN HENRY[7], JOHN B.[6], PETER[5] SCHIRMER II, PETER[4], JOHANN JACOB[3], HANS MARTIN[2], MARTIN[1])* was born March 23, 1911 in Advance, N. C., and died September 16, 1977 in Advance, N. C.. He married (1) ALMA MAE ANDERSON, daughter of JAMES ANDERSON and LILLIE METCALF. She was born 1918 in Yancey County, NC, and died April 24, 1988 in Wake County, NC.

More About ALMA MAE ANDERSON:
Burial: 1988, Advance United Methodist Church Cemetery, Advance, NC

Child of EULIUS SHERMER and ALMA ANDERSON is:

    i.   SUZIE ANDERSON[10] SHERMER, b. May 26, 1953, Davie County, NC; m. DAVID SCHULTZ RAINS, September 10, 1980, Winston-Salem, NC; b. August 27, 1938, Bell County, KY.

Child of EULIUS MERONEY SHERMER is:

    ii.   SUZIE ANDERSON[10] SHERMER.

SUZIE married DAVID SCHULTZ RAINS, September 10, 1980.

15. ATLEE CATON[9] SHERMER *(TANDY MERONEY[8], JOHN HENRY[7], JOHN B.[6], PETER[5] SCHIRMER II, PETER[4], JOHANN JACOB[3], HANS MARTIN[2], MARTIN[1])* was born January 01, 1914 in advance N. C.. She married ERNIE WILLIAM PARSONS.

Children of ATLEE SHERMER and ERNIE PARSONS are:

    i.   PETER[10] PARSONS.

    ii.   NILS PARSONS.

16. LUCY SUSANNAH SYDRENE[9] SHERMER *(TANDY MERONEY[8], JOHN HENRY[7], JOHN B.[6], PETER[5] SCHIRMER II, PETER[4], JOHANN JACOB[3], HANS MARTIN[2], MARTIN[1])* was born November 04, 1916 in Advance, N.C., and died February 13, 1975. She married E. C. MORRISON.

Children of LUCY SHERMER and E. MORRISON are:

    i.   ANN[10] MORRISON.

    ii.   MIKE MORRISON.

17. JEROME QUINTON[9] SHERMER *(TANDY MERONEY[8], JOHN HENRY[7], JOHN B.[6], PETER[5] SCHIRMER II, PETER[4], JOHANN JACOB[3], HANS MARTIN[2], MARTIN[1])* was born July 31, 1919 in Advance, N. C., and died April 24, 1985. He married ERIS ???????.

Children of JEROME SHERMER and ERIS ??????? are:

    i.   TANDY[10] SHERMER.

    ii.   RONALD SHERMER.

    iii.   DONALD SHERMER.

18. JULIA HENRIETTA[9] SHERMER *(TANDY MERONEY[8], JOHN HENRY[7], JOHN B.[6], PETER[5] SCHIRMER II, PETER[4], JOHANN JACOB[3], HANS MARTIN[2], MARTIN[1])* was born June 10, 1922 in Advance, N. C.. She married ???? PATTON.

Children of JULIA SHERMER and ???? PATTON are:
- i. JIMMIE[10] PATTON.
- ii. WILLIAM PATTON.
- iii. JO ANN PATTON.

Generation No. 10

19. MARY REYNOLDS[10] SHERMER *(ANDREW ALEXANDER[9], TANDY MERONEY[8], JOHN HENRY[7], JOHN B.[6], PETER[5] SCHIRMER II, PETER[4], JOHANN JACOB[3], HANS MARTIN[2], MARTIN[1])* was born June 10, 1940 in Richmond, Virginia the old Johnston Willis Hospital. She married WILLIAM BEVERLY LIPSCOMB January 30, 1960 in North Side Baptist Church, Richmond, Va.. He was born December 28, 1938.

Children of MARY SHERMER and WILLIAM LIPSCOMB are:
- i. JULIA[11] LIPSCOMB, b. August 1964.
- ii. JANICE MARIE LIPSCOMB, b. August 19, 1966.
- iii. JASON WILLIAM LIPSCOMB, b. August 06, 1970.

20. CATON ALEXANDER[10] SHERMER *(ANDREW ALEXANDER[9], TANDY MERONEY[8], JOHN HENRY[7], JOHN B.[6], PETER[5] SCHIRMER II, PETER[4], JOHANN JACOB[3], HANS MARTIN[2], MARTIN[1])* was born September 20, 1941 in Richmond, Va. old Johnston Willis Hospital. He married LINDA DIANE ARNOLD March 14, 1960, daughter of THOMAS ARNOLD and PHYLLIS TRAYLOR. She was born September 09, 1941 in Richmond, Va. Grace Hospital.

Children of CATON SHERMER and LINDA ARNOLD are:

21.   i.   SAMUEL ALEXANDER[11] SHERMER, b. October 20, 1960, Richmond, Va. old Johnston Willis Hospital.

     ii.   THOMAS CATON SHERMER, b. September 04, 1963, Richmond, Va. old Johnston Willis hospital.

Generation No. 11

21. SAMUEL ALEXANDER[11] SHERMER *(CATON ALEXANDER[10], ANDREW ALEXANDER[9], TANDY MERONEY[8], JOHN HENRY[7], JOHN B.[6], PETER[5] SCHIRMER II, PETER[4], JOHANN JACOB[3], HANS MARTIN[2], MARTIN[1])* was born October 20, 1960 in Richmond, Va. old Johnston Willis Hospital. He married REBECCA ANNE HOBBS February 11, 1989, daughter of NANCY COFER. She was born December 16, 1960.

Child of SAMUEL SHERMER and REBECCA HOBBS is:
SYDNEY REBECCA[12] SHERMER, b. March 21, 1998.

Here is the line of descent for my wife's paternal side of the family, from the CATON and SHERMER marriages that her line comes from:

CHAPTER 15

Shermer and Caton Families

Descendants of John Caton

Generation No. 1

1. JOHN[1] CATON was born 1705 in Maryland. He married ELIZABETH 1728 in Maryland. She was born 1709 in Maryland.

More About JOHN CATON and ELIZABETH:
Marriage: 1728, Maryland

Child of JOHN CATON and ELIZABETH is:
2.   i.   CHARLES[2] CATON, b. 1733, Maryland; d. 1815, Rowan County, NC.

Generation No. 2

2. CHARLES[2] CATON *(JOHN[1])* was born 1733 in Maryland, and died 1815 in Rowan County, NC. He married JEMMIAH SUMMERS 1755 in Maryland. She was born 1738 in Maryland.

More About CHARLES CATON and JEMMIAH SUMMERS:
Marriage: 1755, Maryland

Child of CHARLES CATON and JEMMIAH SUMMERS is:
3.   i.   JOHN[3] CATON, b. 1758, Maryland; d. 1839, Rowan County, NC.

Generation No. 3

3. JOHN[3] CATON (*CHARLES[2], JOHN[1]*) was born 1758 in Maryland, and died 1839 in Rowan County, NC. He married SUSANNAH.

More About JOHN CATON:
Burial: 1839, Rowan County, NC

Child of JOHN CATON and SUSANNAH is:
4.   i.   JESSE[4] CATON, b. 1780, Rowan County, NC; d. 1860, Rowan County, NC.

Generation No. 4

4. JESSE[4] CATON (*JOHN[3], CHARLES[2], JOHN[1]*) was born 1780 in Rowan County, NC, and died 1860 in Rowan County, NC. He married ELIZABETH ORRELL January 26, 1813 in Rowan County, NC. She was born 1800 in Rowan County, NC, and died 1872 in Davie County, NC.

More About JESSE CATON and ELIZABETH ORRELL:
Marriage: January 26, 1813, Rowan County, NC

Child of JESSE CATON and ELIZABETH ORRELL is:
5.   i.   ALFRED "ALPHA"[5] CATON, b. 1836, Shady Grove, Davie County, NC; d. 1896, Shady Grove, Davie County, NC.

Generation No. 5

5. ALFRED "ALPHA"[5] CATON (*JESSE*[4], *JOHN*[3], *CHARLES*[2], *JOHN*[1]) was born 1836 in Shady Grove, Davie County, NC, and died 1896 in Shady Grove, Davie County, NC. He married MARY ELIZABETH BAILEY February 08, 1854 in Davie County, NC, daughter of SAMUEL BAILEY and MARY CHESHIRE. She was born 1838 in Shady Grove, Davie County, NC, and died Aft. 1800 in Shady Grove, Davie County, NC.

More About ALFRED "ALPHA" CATON:
Burial: 1896

More About MARY ELIZABETH BAILEY:
Burial: Shady Grove, Davie County, NC

More About ALFRED CATON and MARY BAILEY:
Marriage: February 08, 1854, Davie County, NC

Children of ALFRED CATON and MARY BAILEY are:
6.   i.   MINNIE LEE[6] CATON, b. March 03, 1878, Yancey County, NC; d. March 04, 1961, Davie County, NC.
      ii.   LOU E. CATON, b. 1862.
     iii.   SALLIE JANE CATON, b. 1861.
     iv.   ETTA CATON, b. 1866.

Generation No. 6

6. MINNIE LEE[6] CATON (*ALFRED "ALPHA"*[5], *JESSE*[4], *JOHN*[3], *CHARLES*[2], *JOHN*[1]) was born March 03, 1878 in Yancey County, NC, and died March 04, 1961 in Davie County, NC. She married TANDY MERONEY SHERMER 1898 in Davie County, NC, son of JOHN SHERMER and BARBARA HUTCHENS. He was born September 29, 1871 in Yancey County, NC, and died July 18, 1960 in Davie County, NC.

Notes for MINNIE LEE CATON:

E.A. Shermer was a witness at the wedding.

Notes for TANDY MERONEY SHERMER:

Tandy Meroney Shermer served as a Corporal Trooper in Company E, 3rd Cavalry Regiment (Rough Riders) in the Spanish American War. His brother, William Gaston Shermer, served in Company H, 22 Infantry Regiment, as a Corporal in the same War.

More About TANDY MERONEY SHERMER:

Burial: July 19, 1960, Advance Methodist Church Cemetery, Advance, NC

More About TANDY SHERMER and MINNIE CATON:

Marriage: 1898, Davie County, NC

Children of MINNIE CATON and TANDY SHERMER are:

- i. WILLIE JO[7] SHERMER, b. June 10, 1900; m. RICHARD REYNOLDS.
- ii. ANDREW ALEXANDER SHERMER, b. February 15, 1903.
- iii. EDNA SHERMER, b. October 28, 1905; m. ALEXANDER GROSSMAN.
- iv. ALPHIA SHERMER, b. July 01, 1908; m. JOHN VOGLER.
- 7. v. EULIUS MERONEY SHERMER, b. March 23, 1911, Davie County, NC; d. 1975, Davie County, NC.
- vi. ATLEE CATON SHERMER, b. January 01, 1914; m. ERNEST PARSONS.
- vii. LUCY SUSANNAH SYDRENE SHERMER, b. November 04, 1916; m. EDWARD MORRISON.
- viii. JEROME QUINTON "BUCK" SHERMER, b. July 31, 1919.
- ix. JULIA SHERMER, b. June 10, 1922; m. WILLIAM PATTON.

Generation No. 7

7. EULIUS MERONEY[7] SHERMER (*MINNIE LEE[6] CATON, ALFRED "ALPHA"[5], JESSE[4], JOHN[3], CHARLES[2], JOHN[1]*) was born March 23, 1911 in Davie County, NC, and died 1975 in

Davie County, NC. He married ALMA MAE ANDERSON May 28, 1949 in Midway, NC, daughter of JAMES ANDERSON and LILLIE METCALFE. She was born September 01, 1915 in Buncumbe County, NC, and died October 15, 1985 in Wake County, NC.

More About EULIUS MERONEY SHERMER:
Burial: 1975, Advance Methodist Church Cemetery, Advance, NC

More About ALMA MAE ANDERSON:
Burial: October 18, 1985, Advance Methodist Church Cemetery, Advance, NC

More About EULIUS SHERMER and ALMA ANDERSON:
Marriage: May 28, 1949, Midway, NC

Child of EULIUS SHERMER and ALMA ANDERSON is:

    i.   SUZIE ANDERSON[8] SHERMER, b. May 26, 1954, Advance, Davie County, NC; m. DAVID SCHULTZ RAINS, September 10, 1980, Winston-Salem, NC; b. August 27, 1938, Bell County, KY.

        Notes for SUZIE ANDERSON SHERMER:
        Suzie was delivered in Rowan Memorial Hospital May 26, 1953, by Dr. Henry Shaw Anderson.

        More About DAVID RAINS and SUZIE SHERMER:
        Marriage: September 10, 1980, Winston-Salem, NC

AUTHOR'S END NOTES:

I have tried to include only what names and dates could be proved by documentation, so as to have an accurate record of my various family lines. This effort proved to be very difficult, since many of my family did not respond to my queries for information about their in-laws and etc.

Any information in this book may be freely used by any Genealogist, or Historian. It is only as factual as research over a period of two hundred and fifty years can produce. If you find errors, or disagree with my findings, I urge you to do your own research to determine your family roots. SEPARATE DOCUMENTS AS EXHIBITS FOLLOW THIS PAGE.

David S. Rains
Charlotte, NC
June, 2002

DISCLAIMER: This document was prepared for the Henry Rains family of Kentucky, and I have tried to research the sources as well as humanly possible. Like any book or essay dealing with passing time periods of over two hundred years, only so much can be guaranteed to be absolutely true. Documents disappear with age, or fade so much as to be illegible, and memory tends to become fixated on "family legends" and stories. I have taken the sources from old courthouse documents such as marriage, divorce, birth and death records, military records, deeds, land grants and warrants, and burial records.

I have also used much material that was given to me by other researchers and family members, and that were on the WWW. Many of my family members and relations did not return my queries for information, and are therefore missing information on their immediate families, or are included with incomplete information as to marriages, proper names and birth dates, and deaths. I therefore caution you to read carefully and notify me of any mistakes, and I will make the necessary changes.

Thank You to Sue Jones, Yvonne Turner Bice, Trecia Northrup, Linda Goins, Robbie Moye, Melva Wheelwright, Ray Mullins, Terry and Linda Rains, Linda Shermer and all the others who made this research possible. Your help was indispensable and very appreciated!

David S. Rains
Charlotte, NC, February 19, 2002

MISC. LAND DEEDS AND OTHE DOCUMENTS DEALING WITH RAINS:

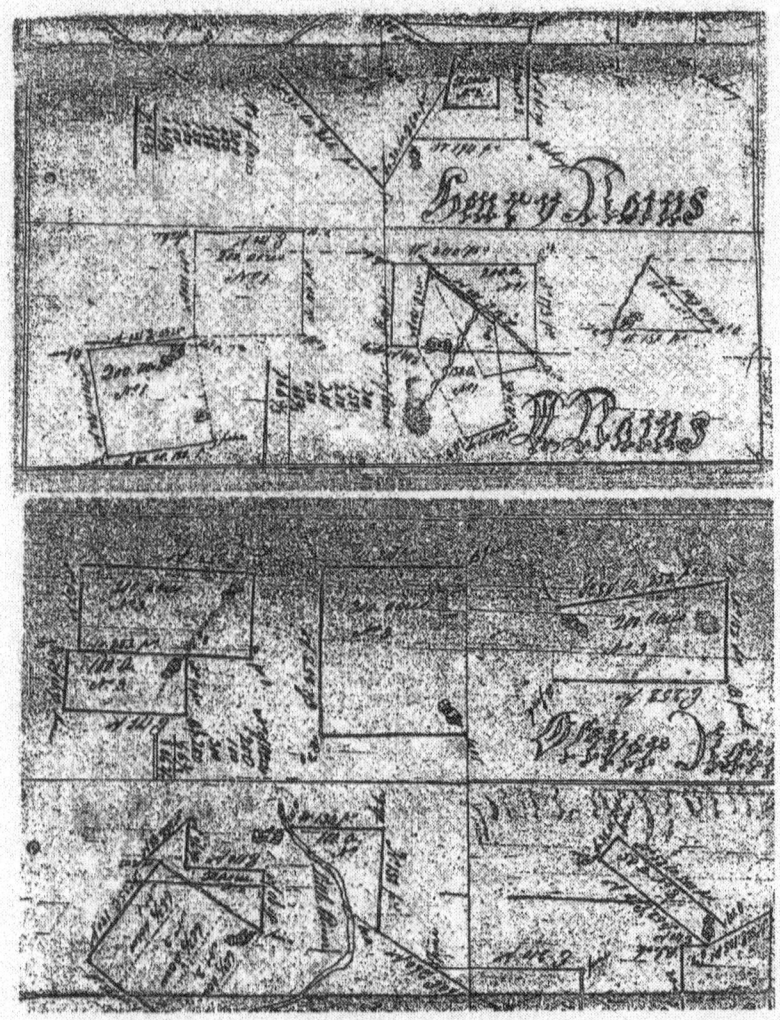

0-595-25655-4